ANTISTHENES FOR BEGINNERS

THE LIFE AND TEACHINGS OF A CYNIC SAGE

BRIAN KOWALSKI

Copyright © 2024 by Brian Kowalski

All rights reserved.

No part of this book may be reproduced in any form or by any electronic or mechanical means, including information storage and retrieval systems, without written permission from the author, except for the use of brief quotations in a book review.

For my Family

There are only two people who can tell you the truth about yourself — an enemy who has lost his temper and a friend who loves you dearly.

— ANTISTHENES

CONTENTS

Introduction   xi

1. **EARLY LIFE AND BACKGROUND**   1
   Birth and Family   1
   Education and Early Influences   2
   Encounter with Socrates   4
   Initial Philosophical Views   5
   Transition to Cynicism   6
   Social and Political Environment   8
   Personal Characteristics and Traits   9

2. **PHILOSOPHICAL FOUNDATIONS**   11
   Definition of Cynicism   11
   Critique of Conventional Values   12
   Emphasis on Virtue   14
   Ascetic Lifestyle   15
   The Role of Self-Sufficiency   17
   Influence of the Socratic Method   18
   Comparison with Other Philosophical Schools   19

3. **MAJOR PHILOSOPHICAL THEMES**   22
   Rejection of Materialism   22
   The Pursuit of Happiness   23
   Concept of Freedom   25
   The Value of Simplicity   26
   Ethics and Morality   27
   Cynic Critique of Society   28
   Practical Applications of Cynicism   30

4. **ANTISTHENES' WORKS AND TEACHINGS**   32
   Key Texts and Fragments   32
   Oral Tradition and Influence   33
   Teaching Methods   34
   Famous Discourses   36
   Influence on Pupils   37

    Legacy of His Writings   39
    Comparison with Contemporary Philosophers   41

5. ANTISTHENES AND SOCRATES   43
    Meeting Socrates   43
    Influence of Socratic Philosophy   44
    Differences from Socratic Thought   46
    Collaboration and Debates   47
    Role in the Socratic Circle   48
    Socratic Method in Antisthenes' Work   49
    Reflections on Socratic Legacy   51

6. ANTISTHENES AND OTHER PHILOSOPHERS   53
    Relationship with Plato   53
    Influence on Diogenes of Sinope   54
    Debates with Aristippus   56
    Critique of Sophists   57
    Interactions with Other Cynics   58
    Antisthenes' Influence on Hellenistic Philosophy   60
    Legacy in Later Philosophical Traditions   61

7. ANTISTHENES' INFLUENCE ON CYNICISM   63
    Founding Principles of the Cynic School   63
    Development of Cynic Philosophy   64
    Key Followers and Disciples   66
    Spread of Cynic Ideas   67
    Differences from Other Cynic Philosophers   69
    Lasting Impact on Western Philosophy   70
    Modern Interpretations of Cynicism   72

8. ANTISTHENES' PERSONAL LIFE AND CHARACTER   74
    Daily Practices and Lifestyle   74
    Public Perception and Reputation   75
    Personal Relationships   76
    Anecdotes and Stories   78
    Antisthenes as a Public Figure   79
    Challenges and Controversies   80
    Death and Legacy   82

9. ANTISTHENES' LEGACY 84
   Immediate Impact on Ancient Philosophy 84
   Influence on Hellenistic Schools 85
   References in Later Philosophical Works 86
   Contribution to Ethical Thought 88
   Role in the History of Philosophy 89
   Revival in Modern Times 90
   Antisthenes in Popular Culture 92

10. MODERN INTERPRETATIONS AND
    RELEVANCE 94
    Contemporary Philosophical Views 94
    Antisthenes in Modern Ethical Debates 95
    Influence on Modern Minimalism 96
    Relevance to Modern Social Critique 98
    Antisthenes and Modern Education 99
    Legacy in Contemporary Philosophy 101
    Future Directions of Antisthenes' Thought 102

Conclusion 105
Glossary 115
Suggested Readings 119

INTRODUCTION

EARLY LIFE OF ANTISTHENES

Antisthenes was born in Athens around 445 BCE. His early life was marked by the influence of both his parents, who provided a nurturing environment. Though not much is known about his childhood, it is believed that he was raised with a strong sense of discipline and curiosity. This foundation laid the groundwork for his later philosophical pursuits. His upbringing in Athens, a city teeming with intellectual activity, played a significant role in shaping his future.

As a young man, Antisthenes showed a keen interest in the world around him. He was not content with the status quo and sought deeper understanding and meaning in life. This quest for knowledge led him to the teachings of various philosophers and thinkers of his time. He was particularly drawn to the ideas that challenged conventional wisdom and societal norms. This early exposure to diverse philosophies helped him develop a critical mind.

INTRODUCTION

Antisthenes' education was not limited to formal schooling. He was an avid learner who absorbed knowledge from various sources. He often engaged in discussions with peers and mentors, always eager to test and refine his ideas. His ability to think independently and critically set him apart from his contemporaries. This intellectual rigor would later define his approach to philosophy.

Despite the challenges he faced, Antisthenes remained committed to his pursuit of knowledge. He understood that true wisdom required patience, perseverance, and an open mind. His early experiences taught him the value of questioning and seeking truth, no matter how uncomfortable it might be. This relentless quest for understanding would become a hallmark of his philosophical journey.

The formative years of Antisthenes' life were crucial in shaping his character and beliefs. His early encounters with different philosophies and his relentless pursuit of knowledge laid the foundation for his later work. These experiences instilled in him a sense of purpose and direction, guiding him toward his eventual role as a pioneering philosopher.

INFLUENCES AND MENTORSHIP BY SOCRATES

One of the most significant influences on Antisthenes was Socrates. Meeting Socrates was a turning point in his life, profoundly shaping his philosophical outlook. Socrates' emphasis on ethics, virtue, and the examined life resonated deeply with Antisthenes. This mentorship helped refine his ideas and sharpen his critical thinking skills.

INTRODUCTION

Socrates taught Antisthenes the importance of questioning and challenging accepted beliefs. Through rigorous dialogue and debate, Antisthenes learned to dissect arguments and uncover underlying truths. This method of inquiry became a central aspect of his philosophical practice. He adopted Socratic questioning as a tool to explore complex ideas and challenge superficial thinking.

The relationship between Socrates and Antisthenes was not just that of teacher and student but also one of mutual respect and admiration. Socrates recognized Antisthenes' potential and encouraged him to pursue his unique path. This support gave Antisthenes the confidence to develop his own philosophical ideas, which would later distinguish him as a founding figure of Cynicism.

Socrates' influence extended beyond intellectual mentorship; it also impacted Antisthenes' lifestyle and values. Antisthenes embraced Socratic simplicity and disdain for material wealth. He believed that virtue and wisdom were far more valuable than riches or social status. This philosophical stance would become a defining characteristic of Cynic philosophy, advocating for a life of virtue and self-sufficiency.

Socrates's mentorship left an indelible mark on Antisthenes. It provided him with a solid foundation in ethical philosophy and critical thinking. The lessons he learned from Socrates not only shaped his intellectual pursuits but also influenced his way of life. This profound impact underscores the importance of mentorship in the development of great thinkers.

INTRODUCTION

FOUNDING OF THE CYNIC SCHOOL

Antisthenes' dissatisfaction with conventional philosophy led him to establish the Cynic School. He sought to create a new philosophical movement that emphasized practical ethics and a return to natural living. The Cynic School rejected materialism and societal norms, advocating for a life of virtue and simplicity. This radical approach challenged the established philosophical traditions of the time.

The founding of the Cynic School was a bold and revolutionary act. Antisthenes' vision was to strip away the superficial layers of society and focus on what truly mattered—virtue and wisdom. He believed that true happiness could only be achieved by living in accordance with nature and rejecting artificial desires. This philosophy attracted followers who were disillusioned with the moral decay of society.

Antisthenes' teachings at the Cynic School were characterized by their practicality and directness. He used everyday examples to illustrate philosophical concepts, making them accessible and relatable. This pragmatic approach distinguished Cynicism from other philosophical schools, which often focused on abstract theories. Antisthenes believed that philosophy should be a guide for living, not just an intellectual exercise.

The Cynic School also emphasized the importance of personal integrity and self-discipline. Antisthenes taught that true freedom came from self-mastery and independence from external influences. This idea resonated with many people who were seeking a more authentic and meaningful way of life. The Cynic School provided a refuge for those

INTRODUCTION

who wanted to escape the corruption and excesses of society.

The legacy of the Cynic School is evident in its lasting impact on Western philosophy. Antisthenes' radical ideas laid the groundwork for later philosophical movements, including Stoicism. The principles of Cynicism continue to inspire individuals who value simplicity, virtue, and authenticity. The founding of the Cynic School was a pivotal moment in the history of philosophy, challenging established norms and advocating for a return to natural living.

CORE PHILOSOPHICAL BELIEFS

Antisthenes' core philosophical beliefs centered around the pursuit of virtue and the rejection of materialism. He argued that true happiness could only be found through living a life of virtue and wisdom. This belief was rooted in the idea that external possessions and societal status were irrelevant to one's inner well-being. Antisthenes' philosophy emphasized the importance of self-sufficiency and independence from external influences.

Central to Antisthenes' beliefs was the idea of living in accordance with nature. He taught that humans should strive to live simply and naturally, free from the artificial desires and distractions of society. This principle was reflected in the ascetic lifestyle that he and his followers adopted. They believed that by minimizing their needs and desires, they could achieve greater clarity and peace of mind.

Antisthenes also emphasized the value of self-discipline and personal integrity. He believed that true freedom came from self-mastery and control over one's desires. This idea was a cornerstone of Cynic philosophy, advocating for a life of restraint and moderation. Antisthenes taught that by mastering oneself, one could attain true independence and inner strength.

Another key belief of Antisthenes was the rejection of conventional social norms and values. He criticized the pursuit of wealth, fame, and power as misguided and detrimental to one's moral character. Antisthenes believed that society's emphasis on material success led to corruption and moral decay. He advocated for a return to simple, natural living as a remedy for these societal ills.

Antisthenes' philosophical beliefs were not just theoretical but also practical. He believed that philosophy should be a guide for living and that true wisdom was reflected in one's actions. This practical approach to philosophy made his teachings accessible and relevant to everyday life. Antisthenes' emphasis on virtue, simplicity, and self-discipline continues to resonate with those seeking a more meaningful and authentic way of life.

RELATIONSHIP WITH OTHER PHILOSOPHERS

Antisthenes had a complex relationship with other philosophers of his time. While he was influenced by many, he also frequently found himself at odds with their ideas. His critical and independent thinking often led to debates and disagreements, particularly with philosophers who held different views on ethics and the good life. These interactions helped shape his own philosophical identity.

One of the most significant relationships Antisthenes had was with Socrates. Their mentor-mentee dynamic was deeply influential, as Socrates' teachings profoundly shaped Antisthenes' thinking. However, Antisthenes also diverged from Socratic thought, particularly in his more radical rejection of societal norms and his ascetic lifestyle. This blend of influence and independence defined much of Antisthenes' philosophical journey.

Antisthenes also interacted with Plato, who was another prominent student of Socrates. Despite their shared heritage, Antisthenes and Plato often clashed. Antisthenes criticized Plato's idealism and theoretical approach, favoring a more practical and grounded philosophy. This intellectual rivalry highlighted the differences between their philosophical perspectives and contributed to the richness of philosophical discourse at the time.

Another notable relationship was with Diogenes of Sinope, who became one of the most famous Cynics. Diogenes was greatly influenced by Antisthenes and adopted many of his teachings. Their relationship exemplified the mentor-mentee dynamic that was crucial in the transmission of Cynic philosophy. Diogenes' radical actions and teachings were a testament to the enduring impact of Antisthenes' ideas.

Antisthenes' interactions with other philosophers were not limited to agreement and mentorship; he also engaged in vigorous debates with those who opposed his views. His critiques of the Sophists and other philosophical schools underscored his commitment to challenging superficial and conventional thinking. These intellectual confrontations helped refine his own ideas and solidify his position as a pioneering thinker.

INTRODUCTION

MAJOR WORKS AND WRITINGS

Antisthenes was a prolific writer, though much of his work has not survived. His writings covered a wide range of topics, reflecting his diverse interests and deep philosophical insights. Despite the loss of many texts, the fragments that remain provide a glimpse into his intellectual legacy. These works are crucial for understanding the development of Cynic philosophy and Antisthenes' contributions to it.

One of Antisthenes' key works was his series of dialogues, which were modeled after those of his mentor, Socrates. These dialogues explored ethical questions and challenged conventional wisdom. Through these writings, Antisthenes demonstrated his ability to engage in rigorous philosophical debate and present complex ideas in an accessible format. His dialogues were influential in shaping the style and content of later Cynic literature.

Antisthenes also wrote extensively on ethics and virtue, which were central themes in his philosophy. His treatises on these subjects delved into the nature of virtue, the importance of self-discipline, and the pursuit of a virtuous life. These writings provided a theoretical foundation for the practical teachings of the Cynic School. Antisthenes' emphasis on virtue as the highest good was a recurring motif in his work.

Another significant area of Antisthenes' writings was his critique of other philosophical schools. He wrote sharp criticisms of the Sophists, whom he accused of being more interested in rhetoric and persuasion than in the pursuit of truth. His polemical works also targeted the materialism and hedonism prevalent in society. These critiques underscored his

INTRODUCTION

commitment to a philosophy grounded in ethical principles and practical living.

Despite the fragmentary nature of his surviving works, Antisthenes' writings had a lasting impact on subsequent generations of philosophers. His ideas were transmitted through his students and influenced later philosophical movements, including Stoicism. The themes and questions he explored in his writings continue to be relevant in contemporary philosophical discourse. His literary legacy is a testament to his enduring influence as a thinker.

HISTORICAL AND CULTURAL CONTEXT

The historical and cultural context of Antisthenes' life was marked by significant social and political changes. Athens, where he was born and lived, was a city-state that had experienced both the heights of cultural achievement and the depths of political turmoil. This environment played a crucial role in shaping Antisthenes' philosophical outlook and his critiques of society.

During Antisthenes' lifetime, Athens was recovering from the Peloponnesian War, which had left the city weakened and politically unstable. The war's aftermath saw a decline in traditional values and an increase in moral and social corruption. This climate of uncertainty and decay provided fertile ground for Antisthenes' Cynic philosophy, which called for a return to virtue and simplicity.

The intellectual environment of Athens was also highly influential. The city was a hub of philosophical activity, home to numerous schools of thought and renowned philosophers. This vibrant intellectual milieu exposed Antisthenes to a variety of ideas and debates, allowing him to refine his own philosophy. The presence of influential figures like Socrates provided both inspiration and challenge, spurring Antisthenes to develop his unique philosophical stance.

Culturally, Athens was experiencing a period of transition. The traditional values and social norms were being questioned and reevaluated. This cultural shift was reflected in the arts, literature, and philosophy of the time. Antisthenes' Cynicism can be seen as a response to this cultural upheaval, advocating for a rejection of materialism and a focus on ethical living. His philosophy was both a critique of contemporary society and a call for a return to more fundamental values.

The historical and cultural context of Antisthenes' life also influenced his reception and legacy. His ideas resonated with those who were disillusioned with the moral decline of society and seeking a more authentic way of life. The challenges and changes of his time provided both the backdrop and the impetus for his philosophical contributions. Understanding this context is essential for appreciating the depth and relevance of Antisthenes' thought.

The environment in which Antisthenes lived was one of both challenge and opportunity. The social, political, and intellectual currents of his time shaped his philosophy and his approach to life. His responses to these influences were not just reactive but also deeply thoughtful and innovative. The historical and cultural context of Antisthenes' life provides a rich tapestry that helps to illuminate his philosophical journey and his enduring impact.

EARLY LIFE AND BACKGROUND

BIRTH AND FAMILY

Antisthenes was born around 445 BCE in Athens, a city known for its rich cultural and intellectual life. His family background was somewhat humble; his father was an immigrant from Thrace, while his mother was an Athenian. This mixed heritage sometimes caused him to face prejudice, as Athenian society could be quite strict about lineage and citizenship. Despite these challenges, Antisthenes would go on to become a significant philosophical figure.

Growing up, Antisthenes was exposed to the diverse cultural milieu of Athens. His father, being an immigrant, brought different perspectives and traditions into their household. This blend of cultures provided Antisthenes with a broader view of the world, which later influenced his philosophical ideas. His early life was marked by curiosity and a desire to understand the world around him.

The family's financial situation was modest, which meant that Antisthenes did not have access to the luxuries that many of his contemporaries enjoyed. However, this lack of wealth did not deter him; instead, it fueled his determination to find meaning and purpose beyond material possessions. His upbringing instilled in him the values of hard work and perseverance, which would later become central to his philosophy.

Antisthenes' relationship with his parents was one of mutual respect and love. They encouraged his intellectual pursuits and supported his desire to learn. This support was crucial, as it provided him with the foundation to explore his interests and develop his own ideas. His parents' open-mindedness allowed him to question established norms and seek out new ways of thinking.

Despite the societal challenges and economic limitations, Antisthenes' early family life played a crucial role in shaping his character. The values and experiences from his childhood would go on to influence his philosophical outlook and his approach to life. These formative years laid the groundwork for his future contributions to philosophy and his role as a pioneering thinker.

EDUCATION AND EARLY INFLUENCES

From a young age, Antisthenes was eager to learn. He attended schools where he was exposed to various subjects, including rhetoric, which was highly valued in Athenian society. His education provided him with a strong foundation in critical thinking and argumentation. These skills would become vital tools in his later philosophical work.

In addition to formal education, Antisthenes was influenced by the intellectual atmosphere of Athens. The city was a hub of philosophical activity, with numerous schools and thinkers contributing to a vibrant intellectual culture. Antisthenes often engaged in discussions and debates with other students and scholars, honing his ability to analyze and critique different viewpoints.

One of the early influences on Antisthenes was Gorgias, a famous sophist known for his skill in rhetoric. Gorgias' teachings on the power of language and persuasion left a lasting impression on Antisthenes. While he later distanced himself from the sophists' relativism, the rhetorical skills he acquired from Gorgias were invaluable. They enabled him to effectively communicate his ideas and challenge others.

Antisthenes was also deeply interested in the works of earlier philosophers, such as Heraclitus and Parmenides. He studied their writings and pondered their insights on the nature of reality and existence. These early philosophical explorations helped him develop a critical mind and a deep appreciation for the complexities of philosophical inquiry.

His early education and influences were not limited to formal teachings and famous philosophers. Antisthenes was also inspired by the everyday people he encountered in Athens. Observing the lives of ordinary citizens and their struggles provided him with a grounded perspective on human nature and society. These observations would later inform his emphasis on practical ethics and the importance of virtue in daily life.

ENCOUNTER WITH SOCRATES

The most pivotal moment in Antisthenes' early life was his encounter with Socrates. Meeting Socrates was a transformative experience that significantly influenced his philosophical trajectory. Socrates' method of questioning and dialogue resonated deeply with Antisthenes, who was already inclined toward critical thinking and self-examination.

Antisthenes became one of Socrates' devoted students, regularly attending his discussions in the Agora. Through these interactions, he learned to challenge assumptions and seek deeper truths. Socrates' emphasis on ethics and the examined life profoundly shaped Antisthenes' views on virtue and the purpose of philosophy. This mentorship provided him with the tools to develop his own philosophical ideas.

The relationship between Socrates and Antisthenes was one of mutual respect. Socrates saw Antisthenes' potential and urged him to follow his own distinct path. Antisthenes, in turn, admired Socrates' wisdom and integrity. This dynamic fostered a rich exchange of ideas and helped Antisthenes refine his thinking. He learned the value of questioning and the importance of living according to one's principles.

Through Socrates, Antisthenes was introduced to a community of thinkers and students who were also grappling with profound philosophical questions. This network of intellectuals provided a stimulating environment for Antisthenes to test and develop his ideas. The rigorous debates and discussions he engaged in during this period were crucial in shaping his philosophical outlook.

Antisthenes' time with Socrates also exposed him to the harsh realities of Athenian society. He witnessed the trial and execution of Socrates, an event that deeply affected him. This injustice reinforced his belief in the need for a philosophy grounded in virtue and ethics, one that could challenge societal norms and promote a more authentic way of living. The influence of Socrates remained a guiding force throughout Antisthenes' life and work.

INITIAL PHILOSOPHICAL VIEWS

Before fully developing his Cynic philosophy, Antisthenes explored various philosophical ideas. His early views were shaped by his education, influences, and his time with Socrates. He was particularly interested in ethics and the nature of virtue, themes that would remain central to his later work. These initial explorations laid the groundwork for his unique philosophical perspective.

Antisthenes believed that virtue was the highest good and that it could be taught and practiced. This belief was in line with Socratic thought, which emphasized the importance of ethical living. However, Antisthenes took these ideas further, arguing that virtue was sufficient for happiness and that external possessions and social status were irrelevant. This radical stance set him apart from many of his contemporaries.

In his early philosophical explorations, Antisthenes was critical of the Sophists, who were prominent in Athens at the time. He rejected their relativism and their focus on rhetoric for its own sake. Instead, he advocated for a philosophy that was practical and grounded in ethical principles. This critique of the Sophists highlighted his commitment to truth and virtue, values that would define his later work.

Antisthenes also began to develop his ideas on self-sufficiency and independence. He believed that true freedom came from within and that individuals should strive to be self-reliant and free from external influences. This emphasis on self-sufficiency would become a cornerstone of Cynic philosophy. His early views on this topic reflected his desire for a more authentic and meaningful way of life.

As he continued to refine his philosophical views, Antisthenes increasingly focused on the practical application of philosophy. He believed that philosophy should not be an abstract exercise but a guide for living. This pragmatic approach distinguished him from other philosophers who were more concerned with theoretical questions. Antisthenes' early philosophical views set the stage for his later development of Cynicism, emphasizing virtue, self-sufficiency, and practical wisdom.

TRANSITION TO CYNICISM

Antisthenes' transition to Cynicism marked a significant turning point in his philosophical journey. This shift was driven by his growing disillusionment with conventional philosophy and societal values. He sought a more radical and authentic approach to living, one that emphasized virtue and simplicity. This transition was not sudden but rather a gradual evolution of his ideas and beliefs.

The influence of Socrates played a crucial role in Antisthenes' move toward Cynicism. Socrates' emphasis on virtue and the examined life resonated deeply with him. However,

Antisthenes took these ideas further, advocating for a complete rejection of materialism and societal norms. He believed that true happiness could only be achieved by living in accordance with nature and embracing a life of austerity.

Antisthenes began to distance himself from the more abstract and theoretical aspects of philosophy. He focused instead on practical ethics and the importance of living a virtuous life. This practical orientation was a defining feature of Cynic philosophy. Antisthenes taught that philosophy should be a guide for living, not just an intellectual exercise. His emphasis on action over theory set Cynicism apart from other philosophical schools.

One of the key aspects of Antisthenes' transition to Cynicism was his embrace of asceticism. He adopted a simple and austere lifestyle, rejecting material possessions and societal status. This asceticism was not just about deprivation but about freeing oneself from the distractions and corruptions of society. Antisthenes believed that by minimizing their needs and desires, individuals could achieve greater clarity and peace of mind.

Antisthenes' transition to Cynicism also involved a critique of conventional social and moral values. He challenged the pursuit of wealth, fame, and power, arguing that these were misguided and detrimental to one's moral character. Instead, he advocated for a return to simple, natural living. This critique of society was a central theme in Cynic philosophy and reflected Antisthenes' desire for a more authentic and meaningful way of life.

SOCIAL AND POLITICAL ENVIRONMENT

The social and political environment of Athens during Antisthenes' lifetime was marked by significant changes and challenges. The city-state had recently emerged from the Peloponnesian War, which had left it weakened and politically unstable. This period of recovery and turmoil provided a backdrop for Antisthenes' philosophical development and his critique of society.

Athenian society was characterized by a rigid social hierarchy and an emphasis on wealth and status. This environment often led to corruption and moral decay, issues that Antisthenes would later address in his philosophy. He was critical of the societal values that prioritized material success over virtue and wisdom. This critique was rooted in his desire for a more ethical and just society.

The political landscape of Athens was also tumultuous. The city experienced periods of democratic rule, oligarchic control, and tyranny. These shifts in governance created an atmosphere of uncertainty and instability. Antisthenes' philosophy of Cynicism, with its emphasis on self-sufficiency and independence, can be seen as a response to this political volatility. He believed that true freedom came from within and that individuals should strive to be free from external influences.

Culturally, Athens was a vibrant center of intellectual activity. The city was home to numerous philosophical schools and thinkers, creating a dynamic and competitive environment. This intellectual milieu exposed Antisthenes to a variety of ideas and debates, allowing him to refine his own philosophy. However, it also led to conflicts and disagreements with other philosophers, particularly those who upheld the conventional values he opposed.

The social and political environment of Athens had a profound impact on Antisthenes' philosophy. His critique of societal norms and his emphasis on virtue and self-sufficiency were responses to the challenges and issues he observed. This context helps to illuminate the motivations behind his development of Cynicism and his desire for a more authentic and meaningful way of life. Understanding this environment is essential for appreciating the depth and relevance of his thought.

PERSONAL CHARACTERISTICS AND TRAITS

Antisthenes was known for his strong character and distinctive traits, which played a significant role in shaping his philosophy. He was a man of great integrity, unwavering in his commitment to his principles. This steadfastness was evident in both his personal life and his philosophical pursuits. He believed in living according to his values, regardless of societal pressures or expectations.

One of the most notable traits of Antisthenes was his simplicity. He lived a life of austerity, rejecting material possessions and luxuries. This simplicity was not just a lifestyle choice but a reflection of his philosophical beliefs. Antisthenes taught that true happiness and freedom came from minimizing one's needs and desires. His own life was a testament to this principle, embodying the Cynic ideal of self-sufficiency.

Antisthenes was also known for his sharp wit and critical mind. He had a keen ability to analyze and dissect arguments, often engaging in rigorous debates with other philosophers. This intellectual rigor was a hallmark of his approach to philosophy. He believed in the importance of questioning assumptions and seeking deeper truths. His critical thinking skills were crucial in developing and refining his own ideas.

Despite his ascetic lifestyle, Antisthenes had a charismatic presence. He was an effective communicator, able to convey complex ideas in an accessible and relatable manner. This ability made his teachings appealing to a wide audience, attracting followers who were disillusioned with conventional philosophy and societal values. His charisma and clarity of thought helped to establish Cynicism as a significant philosophical movement.

Antisthenes' personal characteristics and traits were integral to his philosophy. His integrity, simplicity, wit, and charisma all played a role in shaping his ideas and his approach to life. These traits helped him to live according to his principles and to inspire others to do the same. Understanding these aspects of his character provides a deeper insight into his philosophy and his lasting impact on the world of ideas.

PHILOSOPHICAL FOUNDATIONS

DEFINITION OF CYNICISM

Cynicism is a philosophy that calls for a return to a simple, natural way of living. It rejects the artificial and the superficial aspects of society, urging people to live in accordance with nature. This means living a life of virtue, self-sufficiency, and honesty, free from the distractions and corruptions of wealth, power, and societal expectations. The Cynics believed that happiness and freedom could only be found by embracing these principles.

The term "Cynicism" comes from the Greek word "kynikos," which means "dog-like." This name was adopted by the Cynics because of their shamelessness and their rejection of societal norms. They believed that just as dogs live naturally and without shame, so too should humans. This idea of living without shame was central to Cynic philosophy, as it allowed them to act according to their true nature without being constrained by societal expectations.

Cynicism was not just a theoretical philosophy but a way of life. The Cynics practiced what they preached, living austere and simple lives. They often lived in poverty, with few possessions, relying on their own resourcefulness and the kindness of others. This lifestyle was a direct challenge to the values of wealth and luxury that were prevalent in their society. By living simply, the Cynics aimed to demonstrate the possibility and value of a life lived in accordance with nature.

The Cynics also believed in the importance of honesty and directness. They were known for their blunt and sometimes harsh criticisms of society and its values. This honesty was not meant to be hurtful but to provoke thought and reflection. By speaking the truth, the Cynics aimed to expose the hypocrisy and corruption of their society and to encourage others to seek a more authentic and virtuous way of living.

Cynicism as a philosophy has endured for centuries, influencing various thinkers and movements. Its emphasis on virtue, simplicity, and honesty continues to resonate with those who seek to live a life true to their values. The Cynics' call to live in accordance with nature remains a powerful reminder of the importance of integrity and self-sufficiency in the pursuit of happiness and freedom.

CRITIQUE OF CONVENTIONAL VALUES

The Cynics were known for their sharp critique of conventional values. They believed that society's emphasis on wealth, power, and status was misguided and corrupting. According to the Cynics, these values distracted people from what truly mattered: living a virtuous and meaningful life. They argued that the pursuit of material success led to moral decay and unhappiness.

One of the main targets of the Cynics' critique was the accumulation of wealth. They saw the desire for riches as a source of greed and corruption. In their view, wealth created unnecessary desires and dependencies, leading people away from a life of self-sufficiency and virtue. The Cynics advocated for a life free from material possessions, where one's worth was determined by their character and actions rather than their wealth.

The Cynics also challenged the societal obsession with power and status. They believed that the pursuit of power often led to unethical behavior and exploitation. In their eyes, true power came from within, from one's ability to live according to their principles and values. The Cynics valued personal integrity and self-mastery over external recognition and authority. This perspective was a direct challenge to the power structures of their time.

Another aspect of conventional values that the Cynics critiqued was the importance placed on social norms and conventions. They believed that many of these norms were arbitrary and restrictive, preventing people from living authentically. The Cynics often acted in ways that defied social expectations, such as living in public spaces or engaging in provocative behavior, to demonstrate their rejection of societal constraints. They aimed to show that true freedom came from living according to one's nature, not from conforming to societal expectations.

The Cynics' critique extended to the moral and ethical values of their society. They believed that many of these values were hypocritical and superficial. The Cynics emphasized the importance of genuine virtue, which they saw as being rooted in honesty, integrity, and self-discipline. They challenged others to examine their values and to strive for a more authentic and virtuous way of living.

Through their critique of conventional values, the Cynics sought to provoke reflection and change. They aimed to expose the flaws and hypocrisies of their society and to encourage others to seek a more meaningful and virtuous life. Their critique remains relevant today, as it continues to challenge us to question our values and to strive for a life of integrity and authenticity.

EMPHASIS ON VIRTUE

At the heart of Cynic philosophy is the emphasis on virtue. For the Cynics, virtue was the highest good and the key to a happy and meaningful life. They believed that virtue was not just a theoretical concept but something that had to be practiced and lived. The Cynics taught that true happiness could only be found through living a virtuous life in accordance with nature.

The Cynics' concept of virtue was closely linked to their idea of living in accordance with nature. They believed that humans were naturally inclined towards virtue and that societal influences often led people astray. To live virtuously, one had to strip away the artificial desires and corruptions imposed by society and return to a more natural and simple way of living. This meant focusing on what was truly important: integrity, self-discipline, and wisdom.

The Cynics also emphasized the importance of self-discipline in the pursuit of virtue. They believed that true freedom came from mastering one's desires and impulses. By practicing self-control, the Cynics aimed to achieve a state of inner peace and independence. This self-discipline was not about denying oneself pleasure but about being in control of one's own life and actions. The Cynics taught that a virtuous person was one who could remain steadfast and true to their principles, regardless of external circumstances.

Another key aspect of the Cynics' emphasis on virtue was their belief in the importance of honesty and authenticity. They valued honesty not just in speech but in action and character. The Cynics believed that a virtuous person should be true to themselves and their principles without hypocrisy or pretense. This emphasis on authenticity led the Cynics to reject societal norms and conventions that they saw as corrupting or superficial.

The Cynics' commitment to virtue also involved a focus on practical ethics. They believed that philosophy should be a guide for living and that true wisdom was reflected in one's actions. The Cynics taught that a virtuous life was one that was lived in accordance with ethical principles and that true happiness could only be found through living virtuously. Their emphasis on virtue as the highest good continues to inspire those who seek a life of integrity and meaning.

ASCETIC LIFESTYLE

The Cynics were known for their ascetic lifestyle, which was a direct reflection of their philosophical beliefs. They believed that true happiness and freedom could only be achieved by living simply and minimizing one's desires. This asceticism was not just about deprivation but about finding contentment and fulfillment through self-sufficiency and independence.

Living an ascetic lifestyle meant rejecting material possessions and luxuries. The Cynics believed that these external things were unnecessary and even harmful to one's well-being. They argued that the pursuit of wealth and comfort created dependencies and distracted people from what truly mattered: living a virtuous and meaningful life. By living simply, the Cynics aimed to free themselves from these distractions and focus on their inner development.

The Cynics also embraced asceticism as a way to practice self-discipline and self-control. They believed that by voluntarily giving up comforts and pleasures, they could strengthen their willpower and become more resilient. This self-discipline was seen as essential for living a virtuous life. The Cynics taught that a person who could control their desires and live simply was truly free and independent.

Another important aspect of the Cynics' ascetic lifestyle was their emphasis on self-sufficiency. They believed that individuals should be able to meet their own needs without relying on others. This self-sufficiency was not just about physical survival but also about emotional and psychological independence. The Cynics aimed to cultivate a sense of inner strength and resilience so they could remain steadfast in their principles regardless of external circumstances.

The ascetic lifestyle of the Cynics also involved a rejection of societal norms and conventions. They often lived in public spaces, dressed simply, and engaged in behavior that defied social expectations. This was not just for shock value but to demonstrate their commitment to living according to their principles. The Cynics believed that by rejecting societal norms, they could live more authentically and in accordance with nature.

The ascetic lifestyle of the Cynics was a powerful statement of their philosophical beliefs. It was a way of living that embodied their values of simplicity, self-discipline, and self-sufficiency. Through their ascetic practices, the Cynics aimed to demonstrate the possibility and value of a life lived in accordance with nature. Their example continues to inspire those who seek to live a life of integrity and authenticity.

THE ROLE OF SELF-SUFFICIENCY

Self-sufficiency was a central tenet of Cynic philosophy. The Cynics believed that true freedom and happiness could only be achieved by being self-reliant and independent. This meant not only meeting one's own physical needs but also being emotionally and psychologically independent. The Cynics taught that a self-sufficient person was free from the constraints and dependencies imposed by society.

The Cynics practiced self-sufficiency by living simply and minimizing their needs. They believed that by reducing their dependence on external things, they could achieve greater freedom and contentment. This approach to living was a direct challenge to the materialism and consumerism of their society. The Cynics aimed to show that true happiness came from within and that one did not need wealth or possessions to be content.

Self-sufficiency also involved a focus on inner strength and resilience. The Cynics believed that individuals should be able to withstand external pressures and remain true to their principles. This inner strength was cultivated through practices such as self-discipline, self-reflection, and asceticism. The Cynics taught that a self-sufficient person was one who could maintain their integrity and peace of mind, regardless of external circumstances.

Another important aspect of self-sufficiency was the Cynics' emphasis on personal responsibility. They believed that individuals should take responsibility for their own lives and actions. This meant not blaming others for one's problems or relying on others for solutions. The Cynics taught that true freedom came from taking control of one's own life and being accountable for one's own well-being.

The Cynics also believed that self-sufficiency was essential for living a virtuous life. They argued that dependency on external things and other people often led to compromise and corruption. By being self-sufficient, one could remain true to their principles and live a life of integrity. The Cynics' emphasis on self-sufficiency continues to resonate with those who seek a life of independence and authenticity.

INFLUENCE OF THE SOCRATIC METHOD

The Socratic Method had a profound influence on Cynic philosophy. This method of questioning and dialogue, developed by Socrates, was a central aspect of Antisthenes' approach to philosophy. The Socratic Method involved asking probing questions to challenge assumptions and uncover deeper truths. This approach to inquiry was essential for the Cynics' commitment to truth and virtue.

Antisthenes adopted the Socratic Method as a tool for exploring ethical questions and examining societal values. He believed that by questioning and challenging accepted beliefs, one could gain a deeper understanding of what it meant to live a virtuous life. The Socratic Method allowed

Antisthenes to engage in rigorous philosophical debate and to develop his own ideas through dialogue and reflection.

The Socratic Method also influenced the Cynics' emphasis on honesty and directness. Socrates was known for his straightforward and sometimes provocative questioning, which aimed to expose hypocrisy and superficiality. Antisthenes adopted this approach, believing that honesty and directness were essential for uncovering truth and promoting virtue. This emphasis on honesty was a key aspect of Cynic philosophy.

Another important aspect of the Socratic Method was its focus on practical wisdom. Socrates believed that philosophy should be a guide for living, not just an intellectual exercise. This practical orientation was a central feature of Cynic philosophy. Antisthenes taught that true wisdom was reflected in one's actions and that philosophy should be applied to everyday life. The Socratic Method provided a framework for this practical approach to philosophy.

The influence of the Socratic Method on Cynic philosophy is evident in the Cynics' commitment to questioning, honesty, and practical wisdom. This method of inquiry allowed the Cynics to challenge societal norms and to develop a philosophy that emphasized virtue and authenticity. The legacy of the Socratic Method continues to be a foundational aspect of Cynic philosophy and its enduring influence.

COMPARISON WITH OTHER PHILOSOPHICAL SCHOOLS

Cynic philosophy was distinct from other philosophical schools of its time, yet it also shared some commonalities.

Comparing Cynicism with other schools helps to highlight its unique features and its place within the broader philosophical landscape. One of the key differences between Cynicism and other schools was its emphasis on practical ethics and ascetic living.

Unlike the more theoretical approaches of schools like Platonism and Aristotelianism, Cynicism was deeply practical. The Cynics believed that philosophy should be a way of life, not just an intellectual pursuit. They focused on living according to their principles and demonstrating their ideas through action. This practical orientation set Cynicism apart from other philosophical traditions that were more concerned with abstract concepts and theories.

Cynicism also differed from other schools in its critique of societal values and norms. While many philosophical traditions sought to work within the existing social structures, the Cynics often stood in direct opposition to them. They challenged the importance placed on wealth, power, and social status, advocating for a return to natural and simple living. This radical critique was a defining feature of Cynic philosophy and distinguished it from more conventional schools.

However, there were also some commonalities between Cynicism and other philosophical traditions. For example, Stoicism, which developed later, was influenced by Cynic ideas. Both schools emphasized the importance of virtue and self-control, and both valued living in accordance with nature. The Stoics adopted many Cynic principles but developed them in a more systematic and less radical way. This connection highlights the lasting influence of Cynic philosophy.

In comparison to Epicureanism, Cynicism shared a focus on individual happiness and freedom. However, the two schools had different approaches to achieving these goals. While the Epicureans emphasized the pursuit of pleasure and the avoidance of pain, the Cynics believed in minimizing desires and practicing self-discipline. These contrasting approaches reflect different views on the nature of happiness and the means to achieve it.

Comparing Cynicism with other philosophical schools reveals its unique emphasis on practical ethics, ascetic living, and radical critique of societal values. These features distinguish Cynicism from other traditions and highlight its distinctive contribution to the history of philosophy. The comparison also shows the connections and influences between different schools, illustrating the rich and diverse landscape of ancient philosophical thought.

MAJOR PHILOSOPHICAL THEMES

REJECTION OF MATERIALISM

Antisthenes and the Cynics strongly believed that material possessions were not necessary for a good life. They argued that people often became slaves to their belongings, constantly worrying about acquiring more or losing what they had. This focus on material wealth distracted them from what truly mattered: living a virtuous and fulfilling life. The Cynics saw materialism as a barrier to true happiness and freedom.

In their view, materialism was a form of bondage. People who were obsessed with wealth and luxury were never truly free, as they were always at the mercy of their desires. The Cynics taught that by rejecting materialism, individuals could achieve a state of independence and self-sufficiency. They believed that true wealth came from within and that a simple life free from excess was the path to true contentment.

The Cynics often demonstrated their rejection of materialism through their own lives. They lived simply, owning only what they could carry and finding shelter wherever they could. This ascetic lifestyle was not about suffering but about freedom from the unnecessary complications of wealth. By living with less, the Cynics showed that it was possible to be happy and fulfilled without material possessions.

This rejection of materialism also extended to societal values. The Cynics criticized the way society placed importance on wealth and status, arguing that these values were misguided. They believed that people should be judged by their character and actions, not by their possessions or social standing. This critique of materialism was a central theme in Cynic philosophy and a direct challenge to the values of their time.

The rejection of materialism by the Cynics remains relevant today. In a world where consumerism is rampant, their teachings remind us that true happiness does not come from accumulating things but from living a life of virtue and simplicity. By focusing on what truly matters, we can free ourselves from the endless cycle of desire and find a deeper sense of fulfillment.

THE PURSUIT OF HAPPINESS

For the Cynics, the pursuit of happiness was not about seeking pleasure or avoiding pain. Instead, it was about living a life of virtue and integrity. They believed that true happiness came from within and that it was achieved by living in accordance with nature and one's principles. This idea was in stark contrast to the hedonistic philosophies of their time, which equated happiness with physical pleasure.

The Cynics taught that happiness was a state of mind that could be cultivated through self-discipline and self-awareness. By understanding and controlling their desires, individuals could achieve a sense of inner peace and contentment. This approach to happiness required a deep commitment to personal growth and ethical living. The Cynics believed that by striving to be virtuous, one could find true happiness.

This pursuit of happiness also involved a rejection of external validation. The Cynics argued that true happiness could not be found in the opinions or approval of others. Instead, it came from living authentically and staying true to one's values. This emphasis on internal rather than external sources of happiness was a defining feature of Cynic philosophy.

The Cynics also believed that happiness was not something that could be given or taken away by external circumstances. They taught that individuals could be happy regardless of their situation if they maintained their integrity and focused on what truly mattered. This idea of finding happiness through inner strength and resilience was central to Cynic thought.

The pursuit of happiness, as taught by the Cynics, offers a powerful alternative to the modern obsession with pleasure and success. Their teachings remind us that true happiness comes from living a life of virtue and authenticity. By focusing on our inner development and staying true to our values, we can achieve a deeper and more lasting sense of fulfillment.

CONCEPT OF FREEDOM

Freedom, for the Cynics, was not just about political or social liberty. It was about being free from the chains of desire, fear, and societal expectations. They believed that true freedom came from within and that it could be achieved by living a life of virtue and self-discipline. This internal freedom was seen as more valuable than any external form of liberty.

The Cynics taught that by mastering their desires and emotions, individuals could achieve a state of inner freedom. This meant being in control of one's own mind and actions rather than being driven by external circumstances. The Cynics believed that this self-mastery was the key to true independence and that it allowed individuals to live according to their principles, free from the pressures of society.

This concept of freedom also involved a rejection of societal norms and conventions. The Cynics often defied social expectations, choosing to live simply and honestly rather than conforming to the standards of wealth and status. They believed that true freedom required the courage to be different and to live authentically. This defiance of societal norms was a hallmark of Cynic philosophy.

The Cynics also believed that freedom involved a sense of self-sufficiency. They taught that individuals should rely on themselves and not depend on others for their happiness or well-being. This self-reliance was seen as essential for achieving true freedom, as it allowed individuals to be independent and self-sufficient. The Cynics valued this independence and saw it as a path to a more authentic and fulfilling life.

The concept of freedom, as understood by the Cynics, offers a profound and enduring lesson. In a world where external freedoms can be limited or taken away, the Cynics remind us that true freedom comes from within. By mastering our desires, living according to our principles, and relying on ourselves, we can achieve a state of inner freedom that is unshakable and enduring.

THE VALUE OF SIMPLICITY

Simplicity was a core value for the Cynics. They believed that a simple life, free from unnecessary desires and complications, was the key to true happiness and contentment. This belief was reflected in their ascetic lifestyle, which emphasized living with only what was essential. For the Cynics, simplicity was not about deprivation but about focusing on what truly mattered.

Living simply meant rejecting the pursuit of wealth and luxury. The Cynics argued that these things created dependencies and distractions, preventing individuals from finding true happiness. By living with less, they believed that people could achieve a greater sense of freedom and self-sufficiency. This minimalist approach to life was a direct challenge to the materialism of their society.

Simplicity also involved a focus on inner values rather than external appearances. The Cynics taught that true worth came from one's character and actions, not from possessions or social status. This emphasis on internal rather than external values was a defining feature of Cynic philosophy. It encouraged individuals to cultivate their inner virtues and to live authentically.

The value of simplicity was also evident in the Cynics' approach to relationships and community. They believed that genuine connections were more important than social niceties or status. The Cynics valued honesty and directness in their interactions, and they sought to build relationships based on mutual respect and shared values. This focus on simplicity in relationships was a reflection of their broader philosophical commitments.

The Cynics' emphasis on simplicity offers a powerful counterpoint to the complexities of modern life. Their teachings remind us that true happiness and fulfillment can be found in living simply and focusing on what truly matters. By embracing simplicity, we can free ourselves from unnecessary distractions and dependencies and find a deeper sense of peace and contentment.

ETHICS AND MORALITY

Ethics and morality were central to Cynic philosophy. The Cynics believed that living a virtuous life was the highest goal and that true happiness could only be achieved through ethical living. They argued that morality was not about following rules or seeking approval but about living in accordance with one's principles and values. This emphasis on personal integrity was a defining feature of Cynic thought.

The Cynics taught that ethics was about more than just actions; it was about character. They believed that a truly ethical person was one who cultivated virtues such as honesty, courage, and self-discipline. These virtues were seen as the foundation of a good life, and the Cynics encouraged individuals to develop and practice them in their daily lives. This focus on character and virtue was central to their understanding of ethics.

Morality, for the Cynics, also involved a rejection of societal norms and conventions. They believed that many of these norms were superficial and corrupting, and that true morality required living authentically and independently. The Cynics often acted in ways that defied social expectations, demonstrating their commitment to their principles. This defiance of societal norms was a key aspect of their ethical stance.

The Cynics also emphasized the importance of practical ethics. They believed that philosophy should be a guide for living and that true wisdom was reflected in one's actions. The Cynics taught that ethical living was not about abstract theories but about making ethical choices in everyday life. This practical approach to ethics was a defining feature of their philosophy.

The Cynics' commitment to ethics and morality offers a powerful reminder of the importance of living according to one's principles. Their teachings encourage us to cultivate virtues and to live authentically, regardless of societal pressures. By focusing on character and practical ethics, we can find a deeper sense of purpose and fulfillment in our lives.

CYNIC CRITIQUE OF SOCIETY

The Cynics were known for their sharp critique of society. They believed that many of the values and norms of their time were misguided and corrupt. The Cynics argued that society placed too much importance on wealth, power, and status, and that these values led to moral decay and unhappiness. Their critique was a call for a return to simpler, more virtuous living.

One of the main targets of the Cynics' critique was the pursuit of wealth. They believed that the desire for riches created unnecessary desires and dependencies, distracting people from what truly mattered. The Cynics argued that true happiness and contentment could only be found by rejecting materialism and focusing on inner virtues. This critique of wealth was a central theme in Cynic philosophy.

The Cynics also questioned society's obsession with power and status. They believed that the quest for power often resulted in unethical behavior and exploitation. To them, true power came from within, from the ability to live by one's principles. The Cynics valued personal integrity and self-mastery over external recognition and authority. This viewpoint directly challenged the power structures of their time.

Another key element of the Cynics' critique was their rejection of social norms and conventions. They saw many of these norms as arbitrary and restrictive, hindering people from living authentically. The Cynics often behaved in ways that defied social expectations, such as living in public spaces or engaging in provocative actions. This defiance demonstrated their commitment to living according to their principles.

The Cynics' critique of society was not just about pointing out flaws but about encouraging change. They believed that by challenging societal values and norms, they could inspire others to seek a more virtuous and authentic way of living. Their critique remains relevant today, as it continues to challenge us to question our values and to strive for a life of integrity and simplicity.

PRACTICAL APPLICATIONS OF CYNICISM

The Cynics believed that philosophy should be practical and that its principles should be applied to everyday life. They argued that true wisdom was reflected in one's actions and that ethical living was about making choices that aligned with one's values. This practical approach to philosophy was a defining feature of Cynic thought.

One of the key practical applications of Cynicism was the emphasis on self-discipline. The Cynics taught that by mastering their desires and emotions, individuals could achieve a state of inner peace and independence. This self-discipline was not about denying oneself pleasure but about being in control of one's own mind and actions. The Cynics believed that self-discipline was essential for living a virtuous life.

Another practical application of Cynicism was the focus on simplicity. The Cynics believed that by living simply and minimizing their needs, individuals could achieve greater freedom and contentment. This minimalist approach to life was a way to free oneself from the unnecessary complications and distractions of wealth and luxury. The Cynics demonstrated that it was possible to live a happy and fulfilling life with very little.

The Cynics also emphasized the importance of honesty and authenticity in their practical philosophy. They believed that true happiness came from living authentically and staying true to one's values. This meant being honest with oneself and others and rejecting societal norms that conflicted with one's principles. The Cynics taught that by living honestly and authentically, individuals could find a deeper sense of fulfillment.

The Cynics' practical philosophy also emphasized community and relationships. They believed that genuine connections were more important than social niceties or status. The Cynics valued honesty and directness in their interactions and aimed to build relationships based on mutual respect and shared values. This focus on simplicity in relationships reflected their broader philosophical commitments.

The practical applications of Cynicism offer valuable lessons for modern living. The Cynics remind us that true happiness and fulfillment come from living a life of virtue and authenticity. By focusing on self-discipline, simplicity, honesty, and community, we can find a deeper sense of purpose and contentment in our lives. Their teachings continue to inspire those who seek to live according to their principles.

ANTISTHENES' WORKS AND TEACHINGS

KEY TEXTS AND FRAGMENTS

Antisthenes was a prolific writer, although much of his work has been lost over time. What remains are fragments that offer glimpses into his thoughts and teachings. These fragments, often cited by later philosophers, highlight his emphasis on ethics and virtue. Antisthenes wrote extensively on topics such as the nature of the good life and the importance of self-discipline.

One of the key texts attributed to Antisthenes is his "Heracles," a work that explores the mythological hero's journey as a metaphor for the pursuit of virtue. In this text, Antisthenes uses Heracles' trials to illustrate the challenges and rewards of living a virtuous life. This work was influential in shaping the Cynic philosophy, emphasizing the importance of strength and perseverance.

Another significant work is "Ajax," where Antisthenes discusses the concept of nobility. He argues that true nobility is not a matter of birth but of character. This idea was radical at the time, challenging the traditional Greek view that noble birth determined one's value. Antisthenes' emphasis on personal virtue over hereditary status was a key element of his teachings.

Antisthenes also wrote numerous dialogues modeled after those of his teacher, Socrates. These dialogues often featured conversations with other philosophers and prominent figures of the time, exploring ethical dilemmas and philosophical concepts. Although many of these works have not survived, the fragments that remain demonstrate Antisthenes' skill in argumentation and his commitment to exploring deep philosophical questions.

The fragments of Antisthenes' writings that have been preserved offer valuable insights into his philosophical approach. They reveal a thinker deeply concerned with practical ethics and the pursuit of virtue. These texts continue to be studied and admired for their depth and insight, reflecting Antisthenes' lasting impact on the world of philosophy.

ORAL TRADITION AND INFLUENCE

In addition to his written works, Antisthenes was known for his powerful oral teachings. Much of his influence came from his ability to engage and inspire his students through spoken word. Like his mentor Socrates, Antisthenes believed that philosophy was best communicated through dialogue and direct interaction. His oral teachings were a crucial part of his legacy.

Antisthenes often taught in public places, such as the Agora in Athens. These settings allowed him to reach a wide audience and engage with people from all walks of life. His public discourses were known for their clarity and directness, making complex philosophical ideas accessible to everyday people. This approach was in line with his belief that philosophy should be practical and applicable to daily life.

The oral tradition of Antisthenes also involved a strong emphasis on questioning and debate. He encouraged his students to challenge assumptions and think critically about their beliefs. This method, known as the Socratic method, was central to his teaching style. By engaging in dialogue, Antisthenes helped his students develop their own understanding of ethical and philosophical concepts.

Antisthenes' influence extended beyond his immediate students. His oral teachings were often shared and discussed by others, spreading his ideas throughout Athens and beyond. This broader dissemination of his teachings helped to establish the foundations of the Cynic school of philosophy. The oral tradition played a vital role in preserving and propagating his ideas.

Even though many of Antisthenes' written works have been lost, his oral teachings have had a lasting impact. The ideas he communicated through dialogue and debate continued to influence later philosophers and thinkers. His commitment to the oral tradition ensured that his philosophical legacy would endure, carried forward by those who had the privilege of hearing him speak.

TEACHING METHODS

Antisthenes' teaching methods were distinctive and effective, rooted in his belief that philosophy should be a practical guide to life. He often employed the Socratic method, a form of teaching that involves asking probing questions to stimulate critical thinking and illuminate ideas. This approach encouraged students to engage deeply with philosophical concepts and to develop their own understanding through dialogue.

A typical session with Antisthenes might involve a group of students gathered in a public place, such as the Agora. He would pose a challenging question or present a moral dilemma, inviting his students to explore the issue from different angles. Through a series of questions and answers, he would guide them to uncover underlying assumptions and arrive at deeper insights. This method fostered a dynamic and interactive learning environment.

Antisthenes also believed in leading by example. He lived his philosophy, demonstrating through his actions the principles he taught. His simple and ascetic lifestyle was a powerful illustration of his beliefs about virtue and self-sufficiency. By embodying his teachings, Antisthenes provided a living model for his students to follow. This consistency between his words and actions reinforced the credibility of his teachings.

Another key aspect of Antisthenes' teaching methods was his use of everyday language and practical examples. He avoided complex jargon and abstract theories, focusing instead on concrete situations and relatable analogies. This approach made his teachings accessible to a wide audience, from fellow philosophers to ordinary citizens. Antisthenes' ability to communicate complex ideas in a straightforward manner was one of his greatest strengths as a teacher.

Antisthenes' teaching methods were also characterized by their emphasis on ethical living. He believed that philosophy should not be confined to the classroom but should be applied in everyday life. He encouraged his students to practice what they learned, to strive for virtue in their daily actions, and to live in accordance with their principles. This practical orientation made his teachings relevant and impactful, shaping the lives and characters of his students.

FAMOUS DISCOURSES

Antisthenes was renowned for his engaging and thought-provoking discourses. These public speeches and discussions were a key part of his teaching approach, allowing him to share his ideas with a broad audience. His discourses often addressed pressing ethical questions and challenged conventional wisdom, making them both controversial and compelling.

One of Antisthenes' most famous discourses was on the nature of virtue. He argued that virtue was the highest good and the source of true happiness. This idea was central to his philosophy, and he used his discourse to elaborate on what it meant to live a virtuous life. He emphasized that virtue was not about following societal norms or seeking approval but about living in accordance with one's principles.

Another well-known discourse by Antisthenes focused on the rejection of materialism. He criticized the pursuit of wealth and luxury, arguing that these things led to moral corruption and unhappiness. In this discourse, he used vivid examples to illustrate how material possessions could become a burden rather than a blessing. His call for simplicity and self-sufficiency resonated with many who were disillusioned with the materialism of their society.

Antisthenes also delivered powerful discourses on the concept of freedom. He taught that true freedom was not about external circumstances but about inner independence and self-mastery. In his speeches, he encouraged his listeners to free themselves from the chains of desire and societal expectations. His message was a call to personal liberation and self-discipline, offering a path to genuine autonomy.

One of the most provocative aspects of Antisthenes' discourses was his critique of societal values. He challenged the norms and conventions of his time, questioning the legitimacy of wealth, power, and status as measures of a person's worth. His willingness to speak truth to power made his discourses both influential and controversial. Antisthenes' fearless critique of society inspired others to think critically about their own values and beliefs.

The famous discourses of Antisthenes left a lasting impression on those who heard them. They were not only intellectual exercises but also calls to action, urging individuals to live more authentically and virtuously. Through his discourses, Antisthenes communicated his philosophy in a way that was both accessible and profound, leaving a legacy that continues to inspire.

INFLUENCE ON PUPILS

Antisthenes had a profound influence on his pupils, many of whom went on to become prominent philosophers in their own right. His teachings and example inspired a new generation of thinkers who carried forward the principles of Cynicism. Among his most notable students was Diogenes of Sinope, who would become one of the most famous Cynics in history.

Diogenes took Antisthenes' teachings to heart, living an ascetic and unconventional life that embodied the Cynic ideals. He famously lived in a large ceramic jar and rejected all forms of luxury and societal norms. Diogenes' radical lifestyle and sharp wit made him a legendary figure, and he credited Antisthenes with shaping his philosophical outlook. The master-pupil relationship between Antisthenes and Diogenes is a testament to the enduring impact of Antisthenes' teachings.

Another significant pupil of Antisthenes was Crates of Thebes, who also embraced the Cynic way of life. Crates was known for his generosity and his commitment to living simply. He gave up his wealth to live as a beggar and became a beloved figure in Athens for his kindness and wisdom. Crates' life and teachings further spread the influence of Cynicism, demonstrating the practical applications of Antisthenes' philosophy.

Hipparchia of Maroneia, one of the few female philosophers of the time, was also influenced by Antisthenes. She adopted the Cynic lifestyle and married Crates, sharing his commitment to simplicity and virtue. Hipparchia's participation in the Cynic movement challenged the traditional roles of women in Greek society, showing that the principles of Cynicism were accessible to all, regardless of gender.

Antisthenes' influence extended beyond his immediate pupils to later philosophical traditions. His emphasis on virtue, self-discipline, and practical ethics resonated with Stoic philosophers such as Zeno of Citium. The Stoics adopted many Cynic principles, blending them with their own ideas to create a new philosophical system. This connection between Cynicism and Stoicism highlights the enduring legacy of Antisthenes' teachings.

The impact of Antisthenes on his pupils and subsequent generations of philosophers underscores the significance of his contributions to philosophy. His teachings on virtue, simplicity, and freedom continue to inspire those who seek to live authentically and ethically. The lives and works of his pupils are a testament to the power and relevance of Antisthenes' philosophy.

LEGACY OF HIS WRITINGS

Despite the loss of many of his original works, the legacy of Antisthenes' writings remains strong. The fragments and references that have survived offer valuable insights into his philosophical ideas and their impact on subsequent generations. His emphasis on practical ethics and the pursuit of virtue has continued to influence thinkers and writers throughout history.

Antisthenes' writings were preserved and cited by later philosophers, ensuring that his ideas were not forgotten. Figures such as Diogenes Laertius, who wrote biographical accounts of Greek philosophers, included extensive references to Antisthenes' works. These accounts helped to keep his teachings alive and accessible to future generations. The continued interest in his writings demonstrates their enduring relevance.

The legacy of Antisthenes' writings can also be seen in the development of the Cynic and Stoic schools of philosophy.

His emphasis on virtue and self-discipline laid the groundwork for these movements, which further elaborated on his ideas. The Stoics, in particular, adopted many of Antisthenes' principles, integrating them into their own philosophical system. This blending of Cynic and Stoic thought highlights the lasting impact of his work.

Antisthenes' writings have also influenced modern philosophical thought. The principles of Cynicism, such as the rejection of materialism and the focus on inner virtue, resonate with contemporary discussions about simplicity and ethical living. Scholars and philosophers continue to study his fragments, drawing connections between his ideas and current philosophical debates. The relevance of his teachings in the modern world underscores the timeless nature of his philosophy.

The legacy of Antisthenes' writings is also evident in popular culture. His emphasis on living authentically and challenging societal norms has inspired writers, artists, and thinkers across different fields. The idea of questioning conventional values and seeking a more meaningful life is a theme that continues to captivate and inspire. Antisthenes' writings provide a foundation for these explorations, offering a philosophical framework for understanding and pursuing a life of virtue.

The enduring legacy of Antisthenes' writings is a testament to the power and relevance of his ideas. Despite the loss of many original texts, his philosophy continues to inspire and influence. The principles he articulated and the ethical challenges he posed remain as pertinent today as they were in ancient Greece. The fragments of his writings that survive are a treasure trove of wisdom, offering guidance and insight for those seeking to live a life of integrity and virtue.

COMPARISON WITH CONTEMPORARY PHILOSOPHERS

Antisthenes' philosophy was both influenced by and distinct from the ideas of his contemporaries. While he drew from the teachings of Socrates, his approach differed significantly from other prominent philosophers of his time, such as Plato and Aristotle. Comparing Antisthenes' philosophy with that of his contemporaries highlights the unique aspects of his thought and his contributions to the field.

Plato, one of Socrates' most famous students, developed a philosophy that emphasized the existence of abstract Forms or ideals. Plato believed that these Forms represented the true reality and that the material world was only a shadow of this higher truth. Antisthenes, on the other hand, rejected the notion of abstract Forms. He believed that knowledge should be grounded in the tangible, everyday experiences of life. This practical orientation set him apart from Plato's more theoretical approach.

Aristotle, another major figure in Greek philosophy, focused on the systematic study of various fields, including ethics, politics, and natural sciences. While Aristotle shared some common ground with Antisthenes in terms of ethical focus, he differed in his approach. Aristotle's ethics emphasized achieving a balance between extremes (the "Golden Mean"), whereas Antisthenes advocated for a more ascetic and minimalist lifestyle. This contrast highlights the differing views on how to achieve a virtuous life.

The Sophists, contemporary teachers and philosophers, were known for their rhetorical skills and relativistic approach to truth. Antisthenes was highly critical of the Sophists, accusing them of prioritizing persuasion over truth. He believed that their emphasis on rhetoric and relativism undermined the pursuit of genuine knowledge and virtue. This critique underscored Antisthenes' commitment to ethical integrity and his disdain for superficial arguments.

Another significant contemporary was Diogenes of Sinope, who, although a student of Antisthenes, further radicalized Cynic principles. Diogenes took Antisthenes' ideas to the extreme, living in a large ceramic jar and engaging in provocative public behavior. While Antisthenes laid the philosophical groundwork for Cynicism, Diogenes' actions and lifestyle brought these ideas into sharp relief. The relationship between the two illustrates the evolution and diversification of Cynic thought.

Comparing Antisthenes with his contemporaries reveals the distinctive features of his philosophy. His rejection of abstract theories, emphasis on practical ethics, and critique of societal values set him apart from other thinkers of his time. These differences highlight the unique contributions of Antisthenes to the field of philosophy and his lasting impact on the development of ethical thought. The contrasts and connections between his ideas and those of his contemporaries provide a richer understanding of his philosophical legacy.

ANTISTHENES AND SOCRATES

MEETING SOCRATES

Antisthenes first met Socrates in Athens, a city buzzing with intellectual activity. Athens was home to many great thinkers, but Socrates stood out because of his unique method of teaching through dialogue and questioning. Antisthenes was drawn to Socrates' way of engaging with people, which was different from the typical lectures given by other philosophers.

When Antisthenes began attending Socrates' discussions, he quickly realized that this was a place where his curiosity could thrive. Socrates asked questions that made people think deeply about their beliefs and values. This approach resonated with Antisthenes, who was already interested in exploring the nature of virtue and the good life. The connection between the two grew stronger as Antisthenes saw how Socrates lived his philosophy.

Their relationship developed through countless conversations in the Agora, where Socrates would often be found engaging with anyone willing to talk. Antisthenes admired Socrates' commitment to seeking truth and his disregard for social status. Socrates treated everyone equally, whether they were wealthy aristocrats or humble tradespeople, which left a lasting impression on Antisthenes.

Antisthenes' encounter with Socrates was more than just a meeting of minds; it was a turning point in his life. Socrates' focus on ethics and the examined life provided Antisthenes with a framework to build his own philosophical ideas. The time they spent together discussing and debating was crucial in shaping Antisthenes' approach to philosophy.

The bond between Socrates and Antisthenes was not just intellectual but also personal. Socrates became a mentor and friend, guiding Antisthenes through the complexities of philosophical inquiry. This relationship was foundational for Antisthenes, who would go on to develop his own school of thought, heavily influenced by the teachings and example of Socrates.

INFLUENCE OF SOCRATIC PHILOSOPHY

Socrates' philosophy had a profound impact on Antisthenes, shaping much of his thinking and approach to life. One of the key aspects that Antisthenes adopted was the Socratic emphasis on ethics. Socrates believed that living a virtuous life was the highest goal one could achieve, a belief that Antisthenes took to heart and made central to his own philosophy.

Another significant influence was the Socratic method of questioning. Socrates used this method to uncover deeper truths and challenge assumptions. Antisthenes saw the value in this approach and incorporated it into his own teaching and thinking. By continually questioning and examining, he believed that one could achieve a clearer understanding of virtue and the good life.

Socrates also taught that knowledge and virtue were closely linked. For Socrates, knowing what is right naturally led to doing what is right. Antisthenes embraced this idea, emphasizing that true knowledge involved living out one's principles. Antisthenes stressed this practical application of philosophy in his own teachings.

The influence of Socrates extended beyond methods and ideas to lifestyle. Socrates was known for his simple way of living and his disregard for material wealth. Antisthenes adopted this ascetic lifestyle, believing that true happiness and freedom came from minimizing one's desires and focusing on inner virtues. This simplicity became a hallmark of Antisthenes' philosophy and later the Cynic movement.

Socrates' commitment to living an examined life left a lasting legacy on Antisthenes. The importance of self-reflection and continuous learning became central themes in Antisthenes' own philosophical journey. Socrates' influence was a guiding light for Antisthenes, helping him to develop a philosophy that emphasized virtue, simplicity, and the relentless pursuit of truth.

DIFFERENCES FROM SOCRATIC THOUGHT

While Antisthenes was deeply influenced by Socrates, he also developed his own unique perspectives that diverged from Socratic thought. One of the main differences was Antisthenes' more radical rejection of societal norms and materialism. While Socrates lived simply, he did not explicitly advocate for the complete rejection of material possessions, something Antisthenes later embraced fully.

Another area of divergence was in their views on knowledge. Socrates often professed his own ignorance, claiming that true wisdom was knowing that one knows nothing. Antisthenes, however, believed that certain knowledge was attainable, particularly knowledge of virtue. He argued that through rigorous questioning and self-discipline, one could achieve a clear understanding of how to live a virtuous life.

Antisthenes also differed in his approach to teaching. While Socrates engaged people through dialogue and questioning in public spaces, Antisthenes took a more didactic approach at times, giving direct lessons on ethics and virtue. He believed in the importance of guiding his students more explicitly, helping them to navigate the complexities of philosophical thought and ethical living.

The relationship with other philosophers also highlighted differences. Socrates was known for his ability to engage and challenge a wide range of thinkers, often finding common ground or respectfully disagreeing. Antisthenes, on the other hand, was more critical of other philosophical schools, especially the Sophists. He was outspoken in his belief that many philosophers of his time were more concerned with rhetoric and appearances than with genuine ethical inquiry.

Antisthenes' emphasis on asceticism and self-sufficiency was more pronounced than Socrates'. While Socrates lived modestly, Antisthenes took this further, advocating for a life of minimalism and self-denial. He believed that by stripping away external distractions, one could focus more fully on cultivating inner virtue. This extreme asceticism became a defining feature of the Cynic philosophy, setting it apart from Socratic thought.

COLLABORATION AND DEBATES

Antisthenes and Socrates shared a close intellectual relationship characterized by both collaboration and debate. Their discussions often revolved around fundamental questions of ethics and virtue. Antisthenes valued these debates as they helped him refine his own ideas and challenge his assumptions. The give-and-take of their dialogues was a crucial part of his philosophical development.

Their collaboration was evident in the way they both approached teaching. Antisthenes often participated in Socrates' public discussions, contributing his perspectives and engaging with others. This collaborative environment allowed for a rich exchange of ideas, with each philosopher bringing their unique insights to the table. These interactions were not only educational but also fostered a sense of community among Socratic followers.

Debates between Antisthenes and Socrates were not uncommon. Antisthenes' more rigid views on asceticism and self-sufficiency sometimes clashed with Socrates' more balanced approach to simplicity. These debates were respectful but intense, with both philosophers defending their positions passionately. Such debates were instrumental in pushing Antisthenes to think more deeply about his own beliefs.

The dynamic between collaboration and debate helped Antisthenes to hone his skills in argumentation and critical thinking. Socrates' method of questioning forced Antisthenes to consider different angles and perspectives, strengthening his own philosophical arguments. These intellectual exchanges were vital in shaping Antisthenes' approach to philosophy and teaching.

The collaborative and debate-filled relationship between Antisthenes and Socrates also highlighted their mutual respect. Despite their differences, they recognized the value in each other's perspectives. This mutual respect allowed for open and honest dialogue, fostering an environment where ideas could be freely explored and challenged. The interplay of collaboration and debate between them exemplified the best of philosophical inquiry, where the goal was not to win arguments but to seek truth and understanding.

ROLE IN THE SOCRATIC CIRCLE

Antisthenes held a significant role in the Socratic circle, a group of followers and students who gathered around Socrates to learn and engage in philosophical discussions. This circle was a vibrant intellectual community where ideas were constantly exchanged and tested. Within this group, Antisthenes was known for his sharp mind and strong commitment to ethical living.

As a prominent member of the Socratic circle, Antisthenes often participated in the public dialogues led by Socrates. These sessions were opportunities for rigorous intellectual engagement, where members of the circle would challenge each other and explore complex philosophical issues. Antisthenes' contributions to these discussions were highly valued, as he brought a distinctive perspective grounded in practical ethics.

Antisthenes' role in the Socratic circle extended beyond just participating in discussions. He was also a mentor to younger members, guiding them in their philosophical pursuits. His emphasis on virtue and self-discipline influenced many, helping to shape the ethical outlook of the group. Antisthenes' commitment to living out his principles served as a powerful example for others in the circle.

The Socratic circle was a diverse group, including individuals from various backgrounds and philosophical leanings. Antisthenes' presence added to this diversity, bringing a unique blend of Socratic questioning and Cynic simplicity. His interactions with other members of the circle helped to broaden his own understanding and refine his philosophical views.

Antisthenes' involvement in the Socratic circle also positioned him as a bridge between Socratic thought and the emerging Cynic philosophy. His teachings and lifestyle embodied the principles he learned from Socrates while also pushing the boundaries towards a more ascetic and radical approach. This dual role made Antisthenes a pivotal figure in the transition from Socratic philosophy to Cynicism.

SOCRATIC METHOD IN ANTISTHENES' WORK

The Socratic method, characterized by asking questions to stimulate critical thinking and illuminate ideas, was a cornerstone of Antisthenes' philosophical approach. He adopted this method from Socrates and integrated it into his own teaching and thinking. For Antisthenes, the Socratic method was not just a tool for debate but a way to uncover deeper truths and challenge assumptions.

In his work, Antisthenes used the Socratic method to engage his students and interlocutors in meaningful dialogue. He believed that by asking probing questions, he could help others to reflect on their beliefs and values. This approach encouraged active participation and critical thinking, making philosophical inquiry a collaborative effort. Antisthenes valued the insights that emerged from these dialogues, viewing them as essential for personal and intellectual growth.

The Socratic method also shaped Antisthenes' writing style. His dialogues often featured conversations that explored ethical dilemmas and philosophical concepts. These written works aimed to replicate the dynamic and interactive nature of Socratic questioning, inviting readers to engage with the ideas presented. By presenting arguments in the form of dialogue, Antisthenes encouraged readers to think critically and develop their own understanding.

Antisthenes' use of the Socratic method extended to his public discourses. In these settings, he would pose challenging questions to his audience, prompting them to consider different perspectives and examine their own assumptions. This method was effective in breaking down complex ideas and making philosophy accessible to a wider audience. Antisthenes' ability to communicate through questioning made his teachings both engaging and impactful.

The influence of the Socratic method in Antisthenes' work highlights the importance of dialogue and critical thinking in his philosophy. By adopting and adapting this approach, Antisthenes was able to create a dynamic and interactive form of philosophical inquiry. The Socratic method remained a central feature of his teaching and writing, reflecting his commitment to seeking truth through rigorous examination and thoughtful dialogue.

REFLECTIONS ON SOCRATIC LEGACY

Antisthenes often reflected on the legacy of Socrates and how it influenced his own philosophical journey. He saw Socrates as a guiding figure whose teachings provided a foundation for his own ideas. These reflections were not just about honoring his mentor but also about understanding how Socratic principles could be applied and expanded in new ways.

One of the key aspects of Socrates' legacy that Antisthenes embraced was the focus on ethics and virtue. He believed that Socrates had shown the importance of living a virtuous life and that this was the ultimate goal of philosophy. Antisthenes' own teachings were a continuation of this ethical focus, emphasizing the need for self-discipline and integrity.

Antisthenes also reflected on the method of questioning that Socrates had pioneered. He saw this as a powerful tool for philosophical inquiry and adopted it in his own work. The Socratic method's emphasis on dialogue and critical thinking became a central part of Antisthenes' approach to teaching and writing. He believed that this method was essential for uncovering truth and fostering a deeper understanding of philosophical concepts.

The personal example set by Socrates was another aspect of his legacy that Antisthenes admired. Socrates' commitment to living according to his principles, even in the face of adversity, inspired Antisthenes to pursue a life of simplicity and virtue. This influence was evident in Antisthenes' own ascetic lifestyle and his emphasis on self-sufficiency.

Antisthenes' reflections on Socrates also included a recognition of their differences. While he deeply respected his mentor, Antisthenes was aware that his own approach diverged in significant ways. He took Socratic principles and pushed them further, particularly in his rejection of materialism and his radical asceticism. These reflections highlight the dynamic relationship between teacher and student, where influence and innovation go hand in hand.

Through his reflections on Socratic legacy, Antisthenes acknowledged the profound impact that Socrates had on his life and work. He saw himself as a continuation of Socratic thought, adapting and expanding it to address new challenges and questions. This legacy of ethical inquiry, rigorous questioning, and personal integrity remained a guiding force in Antisthenes' philosophical journey.

ANTISTHENES AND OTHER PHILOSOPHERS

RELATIONSHIP WITH PLATO

Antisthenes had an interesting relationship with Plato, another prominent student of Socrates. While both were deeply influenced by their mentor, their philosophies took different paths. Plato focused on abstract ideals and forms, believing in a higher realm of perfect, unchanging concepts. Antisthenes, on the other hand, was much more grounded, insisting that true knowledge came from practical experience and direct observation.

Despite these differences, there was mutual respect between Antisthenes and Plato. They often engaged in discussions that challenged each other's perspectives. Antisthenes would question Plato's theory of forms, arguing that such abstract ideas were unnecessary for understanding the world. Plato, in turn, would critique Antisthenes' emphasis on practical ethics, suggesting that it lacked depth. These debates were intense but respectful, contributing to the rich philosophical landscape of their time.

Their relationship was not without tension, however. Antisthenes was sometimes critical of Plato's elitism and his tendency to create complex philosophical systems. Antisthenes believed that philosophy should be accessible and useful to everyone, not just the intellectual elite. This critique sometimes led to friction between the two, as Plato saw the value in a more structured and theoretical approach.

Despite their differences, Antisthenes and Plato shared a common goal: the pursuit of truth and virtue. They just had different ideas about how to get there. Plato's idealism and Antisthenes' practical realism provided complementary perspectives that enriched the philosophical dialogue of their time. Their interactions illustrate the diversity of thought that emerged from the teachings of Socrates.

Their relationship is a testament to the vibrant intellectual community in ancient Athens. Through their debates and discussions, both Antisthenes and Plato sharpened their own ideas and contributed to the development of Western philosophy. Their differing views highlight the range of interpretations that can arise from a single philosophical lineage, demonstrating the dynamic nature of philosophical inquiry.

INFLUENCE ON DIOGENES OF SINOPE

Diogenes of Sinope is perhaps the most famous follower of Antisthenes and a prominent figure in the Cynic movement. Diogenes took the teachings of Antisthenes and pushed them to their logical extremes. Known for his ascetic lifestyle and disdain for social conventions, Diogenes became a living embodiment of Cynic principles.

Antisthenes' influence on Diogenes was profound. Diogenes admired Antisthenes' commitment to virtue and simplicity and sought to emulate his teacher's lifestyle. Under Antisthenes' guidance, Diogenes learned to value self-sufficiency and reject material wealth. This foundation enabled Diogenes to develop his own unique approach to Cynicism, one that was marked by extreme austerity and provocative behavior.

Diogenes' famous acts of defiance, such as living in a barrel and carrying a lantern in daylight searching for an honest man, were inspired by Antisthenes' teachings. These actions were designed to challenge societal norms and encourage people to question their values. Diogenes believed that by living a life free from societal constraints, he could inspire others to pursue a more virtuous path.

The relationship between Antisthenes and Diogenes was also marked by a deep mutual respect. Antisthenes recognized Diogenes' potential and encouraged his radical approach to Cynicism. Diogenes, in turn, viewed Antisthenes as a mentor and guide. Their relationship exemplified the teacher-student dynamic that was crucial to the transmission of Cynic philosophy.

Diogenes' life and teachings further spread the influence of Antisthenes. Through his extreme practices and public displays, Diogenes brought attention to Cynic philosophy and inspired many others to adopt its principles. His legacy, built on the foundation laid by Antisthenes, highlights the enduring power of their shared commitment to virtue and simplicity.

DEBATES WITH ARISTIPPUS

Aristippus, the founder of the Cyrenaic school of philosophy, often found himself at odds with Antisthenes. Their debates were a clash of contrasting views on pleasure and virtue. Aristippus believed that pleasure was the highest good and that the pursuit of pleasure was the key to a happy life. Antisthenes, in stark contrast, argued that virtue was the only true good and that pleasure was often a distraction from ethical living.

Their debates were lively and passionate. Antisthenes would challenge Aristippus' hedonistic views, arguing that the pursuit of pleasure could lead to moral decay and dependency. He believed that true happiness came from self-discipline and living according to one's principles. Aristippus, on the other hand, defended his position by claiming that pleasure, when pursued wisely, could enhance one's life without compromising virtue.

These debates were not just theoretical; they reflected the different lifestyles of the two philosophers. Aristippus enjoyed the comforts of wealth and luxury, believing that such pleasures were compatible with philosophical inquiry. Antisthenes, with his ascetic lifestyle, demonstrated his belief that simplicity and self-denial were essential for maintaining virtue. Their differing approaches provided a rich context for their philosophical disagreements.

Despite their differences, there was a level of mutual respect between Antisthenes and Aristippus. They both recognized the other's commitment to exploring the nature of the good life, even if their conclusions were vastly different. Their debates pushed both philosophers to refine their arguments and think more deeply about their own positions.

These interactions highlight the diversity of thought within the philosophical community of ancient Greece. The debates between Antisthenes and Aristippus exemplify how contrasting views can coexist and contribute to a broader understanding of philosophical issues. Their exchanges were a testament to the dynamic and evolving nature of philosophical inquiry.

CRITIQUE OF SOPHISTS

Antisthenes was highly critical of the Sophists, a group of itinerant teachers who were known for their rhetorical skills and relativistic approach to truth. He believed that the Sophists were more interested in winning arguments and making money than in seeking genuine knowledge and virtue. This critique was central to his philosophy and teaching.

One of Antisthenes' main criticisms of the Sophists was their emphasis on rhetoric over substance. The Sophists were skilled in the art of persuasion, often using elaborate arguments to convince others of their point of view. Antisthenes saw this as a superficial approach to philosophy, one that prioritized style over truth. He argued that true philosophy required rigorous thinking and a commitment to ethical principles.

Antisthenes also took issue with the Sophists' relativism. The Sophists often taught that truth was subjective and that different people could have different truths. Antisthenes believed this undermined the pursuit of objective knowledge and virtue. He argued that there were universal truths about ethics and the good life that could be discovered through reason and reflection.

The critique of the Sophists extended to their role in society. Antisthenes believed that the Sophists were contributing to moral decay by promoting a relativistic and cynical view of truth. He saw them as charlatans who were more interested in their own gain than in the well-being of their students. This critique was part of a broader rejection of materialism and self-interest that characterized Antisthenes' philosophy.

Antisthenes' opposition to the Sophists was a defining feature of his philosophical identity. It set him apart from other thinkers of his time and reinforced his commitment to a philosophy grounded in virtue and integrity. This critique also helped to shape the development of Cynic philosophy, which emphasized simplicity, honesty, and the rejection of superficial values.

INTERACTIONS WITH OTHER CYNICS

Antisthenes' interactions with other Cynics were crucial in shaping the development of the Cynic school of philosophy. As one of the founding figures, Antisthenes played a key role in mentoring and guiding other Cynics. His teachings and example provided a foundation for the movement, influencing how Cynicism evolved over time.

One of the most significant interactions was with Diogenes of Sinope, who took Cynic principles to their extreme. Antisthenes' emphasis on virtue and simplicity deeply influenced Diogenes, who became known for his radical lifestyle and public provocations. This relationship exemplified the mentor-student dynamic that was central to the transmission of Cynic ideas.

Antisthenes also interacted with Crates of Thebes, another prominent Cynic. Crates was known for his generosity and his commitment to living a life free from material possessions. Under Antisthenes' influence, Crates embraced the Cynic ideals of self-sufficiency and ethical living. Crates' life and teachings further spread Cynic philosophy, demonstrating its practical applications.

Hipparchia of Maroneia, one of the few female philosophers of the time, also came under Antisthenes' influence. She adopted the Cynic lifestyle and became a significant figure in the movement. Her participation challenged traditional gender roles and highlighted the inclusive nature of Cynic philosophy. Antisthenes' interactions with Hipparchia showed that Cynicism was accessible to all, regardless of gender.

These interactions with other Cynics highlight the collaborative nature of the movement. Antisthenes' teachings provided a common foundation, but each individual Cynic interpreted and applied these principles in their own way. This diversity within the movement enriched Cynic philosophy and ensured its enduring influence.

The relationships between Antisthenes and other Cynics demonstrate the importance of mentorship and community in the development of philosophical ideas. Through these interactions, Cynic philosophy evolved and adapted, remaining relevant and impactful across different contexts and generations.

ANTISTHENES' INFLUENCE ON HELLENISTIC PHILOSOPHY

Antisthenes' influence extended beyond the Cynic movement, impacting the broader landscape of Hellenistic philosophy. His emphasis on virtue, simplicity, and self-discipline resonated with many thinkers of the time and helped shape the development of other philosophical schools, most notably Stoicism.

Stoic philosophy, founded by Zeno of Citium, drew heavily on Cynic principles. Zeno studied under Crates of Thebes, who was himself influenced by Antisthenes. The Stoics adopted the Cynic emphasis on living according to nature and practicing self-discipline. However, they developed these ideas into a more systematic philosophical framework, integrating them with other concepts such as logic and natural law.

Antisthenes' focus on practical ethics also influenced the ethical teachings of Stoicism. The Stoics believed that virtue was the highest good and that living a virtuous life was essential for achieving inner peace and happiness. This ethical orientation was a direct continuation of Antisthenes' teachings, demonstrating his lasting impact on the development of ethical thought.

The influence of Antisthenes can also be seen in the works of later Hellenistic philosophers such as Epictetus and Marcus Aurelius. These thinkers emphasized the importance of self-control, resilience, and living in accordance with one's principles. Their writings reflect the enduring legacy of Antisthenes' emphasis on virtue and practical wisdom.

Beyond Stoicism, Antisthenes' ideas contributed to the broader discourse on ethics and the good life in Hellenistic philosophy. His rejection of materialism and his focus on inner virtue challenged other philosophical schools to reconsider their own positions. This critical engagement enriched the philosophical debates of the time and ensured that Antisthenes' ideas remained influential.

Antisthenes' impact on Hellenistic philosophy highlights the interconnectedness of philosophical traditions. His teachings provided a foundation for subsequent developments, demonstrating the dynamic and evolving nature of philosophical inquiry. The enduring influence of his ideas underscores the significance of his contributions to the history of philosophy.

LEGACY IN LATER PHILOSOPHICAL TRADITIONS

Antisthenes' legacy extends far beyond his own time, influencing a wide range of later philosophical traditions. His emphasis on virtue, simplicity, and self-discipline has resonated with thinkers across different cultures and eras, demonstrating the timeless relevance of his ideas.

In the Roman world, the influence of Antisthenes can be seen in the works of Stoic philosophers such as Seneca and Marcus Aurelius. These thinkers adopted and adapted Cynic principles, integrating them into their own philosophical systems. The Stoic emphasis on ethical living, resilience, and inner peace reflects the enduring impact of Antisthenes' teachings on Roman philosophy.

During the Renaissance, the revival of interest in classical philosophy brought renewed attention to Antisthenes and the Cynics. Humanist scholars explored the ethical teachings of the Cynics, finding inspiration in their emphasis on virtue and moral integrity. This period saw a resurgence of interest in Cynic philosophy, demonstrating its continued relevance in different historical contexts.

In modern times, the principles of Cynicism have found new expression in various philosophical and social movements. The emphasis on simplicity and rejection of materialism resonates with contemporary minimalism and anti-consumerist ideologies. Thinkers such as Henry David Thoreau and Mahatma Gandhi have drawn on Cynic principles in their own advocacy for simple living and ethical integrity.

Antisthenes' legacy also extends to existentialist and postmodern philosophies. The Cynic emphasis on living authentically and challenging societal norms has parallels in the existentialist focus on individual freedom and authenticity. Postmodern critiques of consumerism and superficiality echo the Cynic rejection of materialism and conventional values.

The lasting influence of Antisthenes' ideas is a testament to the power and relevance of his philosophy. His teachings on virtue, simplicity, and ethical living continue to inspire and challenge thinkers across different eras and cultures. The enduring legacy of Antisthenes highlights the timeless nature of his contributions to philosophy and the ongoing importance of his insights in the pursuit of a meaningful and virtuous life.

ANTISTHENES' INFLUENCE ON CYNICISM

FOUNDING PRINCIPLES OF THE CYNIC SCHOOL

Antisthenes is often seen as the founder of the Cynic school of philosophy. His teachings centered around a few key principles that would become the foundation of Cynic thought. First and foremost was the idea that virtue was the only true good. Antisthenes believed that living a virtuous life was the most important goal one could have and that everything else, like wealth or fame, was secondary.

Another principle was self-sufficiency. Antisthenes taught that true happiness came from being independent and not relying on external things. He believed that people should learn to be content with what they have and not constantly seek more. This idea of self-sufficiency was closely tied to his belief in living a simple life free from the distractions of material possessions.

Living according to nature was also a key principle. Antisthenes believed that people should live in a way that was natural and not influenced by the artificial norms of society. This meant rejecting societal expectations and living in a way that was true to oneself. For Antisthenes, living naturally was the path to true freedom and happiness.

Antisthenes also emphasized the importance of self-discipline. He believed that to live a virtuous and self-sufficient life, one needed to have control over their desires and impulses. Self-discipline was seen as essential for achieving the kind of life Antisthenes advocated for. This included not only controlling one's desires for material things but also maintaining control over one's emotions and reactions.

These founding principles—virtue, self-sufficiency, living according to nature, and self-discipline—formed the core of Cynic philosophy. They were not just abstract ideas but practical guidelines for living. Antisthenes' teachings provided a framework that his followers could apply to their everyday lives, making Cynicism a lived philosophy rather than just a theoretical one.

DEVELOPMENT OF CYNIC PHILOSOPHY

After Antisthenes, the Cynic philosophy continued to evolve. His followers took his ideas and expanded on them, sometimes in new and unexpected ways. One of the most famous of these followers was Diogenes of Sinope, who took Cynic principles to their extremes. Diogenes lived in a barrel and famously walked around Athens during the day with a lantern, claiming to be looking for an honest man.

Diogenes' lifestyle was a direct reflection of Cynic values. He lived with almost no possessions, relying on his wits and the kindness of strangers to survive. His actions were meant to challenge societal norms and show that true happiness did not come from material wealth or social status. Diogenes' extreme asceticism highlighted the practical application of Cynic principles in a very visible way.

Crates of Thebes was another key figure in the development of Cynic philosophy. Unlike Diogenes, Crates was known for his kindness and generosity. He gave away his wealth to live a life of poverty and simplicity, teaching others about Cynic values. Crates' approach was more compassionate, focusing on helping others understand and adopt Cynic principles. His teachings helped spread Cynicism more widely.

Hipparchia of Maroneia, one of the few female philosophers of the time, also contributed to the development of Cynic thought. She married Crates and adopted the Cynic lifestyle, challenging traditional gender roles. Hipparchia's involvement in the Cynic movement showed that its principles were accessible to everyone, regardless of gender. Her participation added a new dimension to Cynic philosophy, emphasizing its inclusiveness.

The development of Cynic philosophy was marked by diversity in practice and interpretation. While all Cynics adhered to the core principles laid out by Antisthenes, they each brought their own perspectives and approaches to the philosophy. This diversity helped Cynicism remain a dynamic and evolving tradition, capable of adapting to new challenges and contexts while staying true to its foundational ideas.

KEY FOLLOWERS AND DISCIPLES

Antisthenes' teachings inspired a number of key followers and disciples who played crucial roles in spreading and developing Cynic philosophy. These individuals each brought their unique perspectives and practices to the movement, enriching its diversity and influence.

Diogenes of Sinope is perhaps the most famous of Antisthenes' followers. Known for his extreme ascetic lifestyle, Diogenes became a legendary figure in Cynic philosophy. His provocative actions, like living in a barrel and carrying a lantern in daylight, were meant to challenge societal norms and provoke thought. Diogenes' commitment to living according to nature and rejecting materialism embodied the core principles of Cynicism in a very visible way.

Crates of Thebes, another prominent disciple, took a different approach. He was known for his generosity and kindness. Crates gave up his wealth to live a life of poverty, teaching others about the values of simplicity and virtue. His approach was more compassionate and educational, helping to spread Cynic ideas through his teachings and example. Crates' influence extended to notable figures like Zeno of Citium, who would go on to found Stoicism.

Hipparchia of Maroneia, Crates' wife, was a significant figure in her own right. She adopted the Cynic lifestyle and philosophy, challenging traditional gender roles. Hipparchia's involvement in the Cynic movement highlighted its inclusiveness and the relevance of its principles to all people, regardless of gender. Her participation added depth to the movement and demonstrated the practical application of Cynic ideas in everyday life.

Menippus, another follower, contributed to the spread of Cynic ideas through his satirical writings. His works often mocked societal norms and highlighted the absurdities of human behavior. Menippus' use of humor and satire made Cynic philosophy more accessible and engaging to a broader audience, further spreading its influence.

The key followers and disciples of Antisthenes each played a vital role in the evolution and dissemination of Cynic philosophy. Their diverse approaches and contributions enriched the movement and ensured its continued relevance. The legacy of these followers demonstrates the enduring appeal and adaptability of Cynic thought, which has inspired and challenged thinkers across different eras and cultures.

SPREAD OF CYNIC IDEAS

The spread of Cynic philosophy was driven by the dedicated efforts of Antisthenes' followers, who traveled widely and shared Cynic principles through teaching, writing, and public demonstration. Their efforts helped to ensure that Cynic ideas reached a broad audience and left a lasting impact.

Diogenes of Sinope's radical lifestyle and public acts of defiance drew significant attention to Cynic philosophy. His reputation as a living embodiment of Cynic principles made him a well-known figure across Greece. Diogenes' provocative actions and sharp wit challenged societal norms and sparked interest in the Cynic way of life. His influence helped to spread Cynic ideas to a broader audience.

Crates of Thebes also played a key role in the dissemination of Cynic thought. By renouncing his wealth and living a life of poverty, Crates provided a powerful example of Cynic principles in action. His teachings attracted many followers, including Zeno of Citium, who would go on to found the Stoic school of philosophy. Through Crates and his students, Cynic ideas spread to new regions and influenced other philosophical traditions.

The writings of Cynic philosophers were another important vehicle for spreading their ideas. While much of their work has been lost, the fragments that remain show a commitment to practical ethics and sharp critique of societal values. Menippus, for instance, used satire to convey Cynic principles, making philosophy accessible and engaging to a wider audience. These writings helped to disseminate Cynic thought and ensured its enduring influence.

Cynic philosophy also spread through direct interaction with other cultures. Onesicritus, a student of Diogenes, accompanied Alexander the Great on his campaigns and introduced Cynic ideas to the East. This interaction facilitated a cross-pollination of philosophical traditions, enriching both Cynicism and the cultures it encountered. The spread of Cynic ideas beyond Greece demonstrated their universal appeal and adaptability.

The spread of Cynic philosophy was not limited to the ancient world. Throughout history, Cynic principles have continued to resonate with those seeking a life of virtue and simplicity. The enduring influence of Cynicism is evident in various philosophical and cultural movements, reflecting the timeless relevance of its core principles.

DIFFERENCES FROM OTHER CYNIC PHILOSOPHERS

While Antisthenes laid the foundation for Cynic philosophy, his followers often interpreted and applied his principles in diverse and sometimes contrasting ways. These differences highlight the flexibility and adaptability of Cynic thought, which allowed it to evolve and respond to new challenges and contexts.

Diogenes of Sinope, for example, took Cynic principles to their extreme. His lifestyle was marked by radical asceticism and public provocations. Diogenes believed in living in complete harmony with nature, free from all societal constraints. His approach was more confrontational and provocative than Antisthenes', often using shocking behavior to challenge societal norms and provoke thought. This radical interpretation made Diogenes a controversial but highly influential figure.

In contrast, Crates of Thebes adopted a more compassionate and educational approach. While he also embraced poverty and simplicity, Crates focused on teaching and helping others understand Cynic principles. He believed in the importance of community and shared learning, which set him apart from Diogenes' more individualistic and confrontational style. Crates' approach helped to spread Cynic philosophy more widely and attract a broader range of followers.

Hipparchia of Maroneia's contribution also highlighted differences within Cynic thought. As one of the few female philosophers of the time, she challenged traditional gender roles and demonstrated the inclusive nature of Cynic principles. Hipparchia's involvement brought a new perspective to Cynicism, emphasizing the relevance of its principles to all people, regardless of gender. Her unique contribution enriched the Cynic movement and demonstrated its adaptability.

Menippus, another prominent Cynic, used satire and humor to convey philosophical ideas. His writings often mocked societal norms and pretensions, making Cynic principles accessible and engaging. Menippus' approach differed from the more austere methods of Antisthenes and Diogenes, showing that Cynic philosophy could be expressed in various forms, including literature and satire. This diversity of expression helped to broaden the appeal of Cynic thought.

These differences among Cynic philosophers highlight the movement's dynamic and evolving nature. While they all adhered to the core principles of virtue, simplicity, and self-sufficiency, their diverse approaches enriched Cynic philosophy and ensured its continued relevance. The ability to adapt and reinterpret its principles allowed Cynicism to thrive and influence a wide range of thinkers and traditions.

LASTING IMPACT ON WESTERN PHILOSOPHY

The influence of Cynic philosophy extends far beyond its origins in ancient Greece, leaving a lasting impact on Western thought. The core principles established by Antisthenes—virtue, simplicity, and self-sufficiency—have continued to inspire and challenge philosophers throughout history. The enduring legacy of Cynic thought is evident in its influence on various philosophical traditions.

One of the most significant impacts of Cynic philosophy is its influence on Stoicism. Zeno of Citium, the founder of Stoicism, was a student of Crates of Thebes, a key figure in the Cynic movement. The Stoic emphasis on living in accordance with nature, practicing self-discipline, and focusing on inner virtue reflects the foundational principles of Cynicism. Stoicism built upon Cynic ideas, integrating them into a more systematic philosophical framework that has had a profound impact on Western thought.

Cynic philosophy also influenced the development of early Christian thought. The emphasis on asceticism, self-denial, and rejection of material wealth found in Cynic teachings resonated with early Christian values. Many early Christian thinkers, including the Desert Fathers, adopted Cynic practices of simplicity and asceticism as a means of spiritual purification. This influence helped to shape the ethical and ascetic traditions within Christianity.

During the Renaissance, the revival of classical learning brought renewed interest in Cynic philosophy. Humanist scholars explored the ethical teachings of the Cynics, finding inspiration in their commitment to virtue and moral integrity. The emphasis on practical ethics and living a life of simplicity and virtue influenced Renaissance thought and contributed to the broader intellectual movement of the time.

In modern times, the principles of Cynicism continue to resonate with contemporary philosophical and cultural movements. The focus on simplicity, authenticity, and ethical living has parallels in movements such as minimalism and environmentalism. Thinkers like Henry David Thoreau and contemporary advocates for simple living draw on

Cynic principles in their critiques of consumerism and their calls for a return to a more natural and virtuous way of life.

The lasting impact of Cynic philosophy on Western thought is a testament to the enduring relevance of its core principles. The emphasis on virtue, simplicity, and self-sufficiency continues to inspire and challenge thinkers across different eras and cultures. The legacy of Cynic thought highlights the timeless nature of its insights and its continued importance in the pursuit of a meaningful and ethical life.

MODERN INTERPRETATIONS OF CYNICISM

In the modern world, Cynicism has taken on new meanings and interpretations. While the term "cynic" often carries a negative connotation today, associated with skepticism and distrust, the philosophical roots of Cynicism remain relevant and influential. Contemporary interpretations of Cynic philosophy reflect its enduring appeal and adaptability to modern challenges.

One area where Cynic principles have found a new expression is in the minimalist movement. Modern minimalists advocate for living with fewer possessions and focusing on what truly matters, echoing the Cynic emphasis on simplicity and self-sufficiency. The rejection of consumerism and the pursuit of a more meaningful life through minimalism resonate with the core tenets of Cynic philosophy.

Environmentalism is another field where Cynic ideas have found a modern application. The emphasis on living in accordance with nature and rejecting material excess aligns with contemporary efforts to promote sustainable living. Environmental activists draw on Cynic principles to advocate for a lifestyle that minimizes harm to the environment and prioritizes ethical living.

In the realm of psychology, the focus on authenticity and self-awareness in Cynic philosophy has parallels with modern therapeutic practices. The emphasis on living true to one's values and rejecting societal pressures is reflected in approaches such as existential therapy and mindfulness. These practices encourage individuals to cultivate inner strength and resilience, much like the Cynics' focus on self-discipline and self-mastery.

The influence of Cynic principles is also evident in contemporary critiques of societal norms and institutions. Modern social critics often challenge the status quo, questioning the values and practices of mainstream society. This critical stance is in line with the Cynic tradition of questioning and defying social conventions to promote a more authentic and ethical way of life.

Despite the negative connotations often associated with the term "cynic," the philosophical principles established by Antisthenes continue to offer valuable insights for modern living. The focus on virtue, simplicity, and self-sufficiency remains relevant in addressing contemporary challenges. By drawing on the timeless wisdom of Cynic philosophy, modern thinkers and practitioners can find guidance in the pursuit of a meaningful and virtuous life.

ANTISTHENES' PERSONAL LIFE AND CHARACTER

DAILY PRACTICES AND LIFESTYLE

Antisthenes lived a life that reflected his philosophical beliefs. He believed in simplicity, so his daily practices were minimalistic. He owned very few possessions, believing that material wealth was unnecessary for a happy life. His lifestyle was a testament to his philosophy that virtue and self-sufficiency were the keys to a good life.

Every morning, Antisthenes would wake up early and meditate on his principles. He would think about virtue, the importance of living naturally, and the value of self-discipline. This practice helped him stay focused on his goals and maintain his commitment to living a virtuous life. Meditation was an essential part of his routine, allowing him to reflect and prepare for the day ahead.

Antisthenes also believed in physical activity. He would spend part of his day exercising, which he thought was crucial for maintaining a healthy body and mind. This could involve simple exercises like walking or more rigorous activities. By keeping his body fit, Antisthenes believed he could better focus on his philosophical pursuits.

His diet was simple, consisting mostly of basic, unprocessed foods. Antisthenes believed that eating simply was another way to practice self-discipline and avoid the distractions of indulgence. He would often eat only what was necessary to sustain himself, avoiding any luxuries or excesses. This simple diet was part of his broader commitment to living in harmony with nature.

Throughout the day, Antisthenes would engage with others, often discussing philosophy in public places like the Agora. He enjoyed sharing his ideas and debating with others, seeing these interactions as opportunities to teach and learn. His public discussions were a vital part of his daily life, reflecting his belief that philosophy should be practiced openly and actively.

PUBLIC PERCEPTION AND REPUTATION

Antisthenes was a well-known figure in Athens, and his lifestyle and beliefs garnered much attention. To some, he was a respected philosopher who lived by his principles. They admired his commitment to simplicity and virtue, seeing him as a role model. His teachings attracted many followers who were inspired by his dedication and integrity.

However, not everyone viewed Antisthenes so positively. Some people saw his rejection of material wealth and societal norms as strange or even foolish. They did not understand why he would choose to live with so little when he could have had much more. His radical ideas about self-sufficiency and rejecting conventional values were controversial and challenged the status quo.

Despite the mixed opinions, Antisthenes' reputation as a thinker was well-established. He was known for his sharp mind and his ability to debate complex philosophical ideas. His public discussions were often lively and thought-provoking, attracting people who were curious about his views. Even those who disagreed with him acknowledged his intellectual prowess and his commitment to his beliefs.

Antisthenes also had a reputation for being blunt and direct. He did not shy away from criticizing others, especially those he saw as hypocritical or superficial. This honesty was both a strength and a weakness; while it made him a powerful critic, it also alienated some people. His uncompromising nature meant that he often stood alone, unafraid to voice unpopular opinions.

Over time, Antisthenes' reputation grew beyond Athens. His teachings and lifestyle became known in other parts of Greece, influencing a broader audience. His impact was felt not just through his direct followers but also through the way he challenged societal norms and inspired others to think more deeply about the meaning of a virtuous life.

PERSONAL RELATIONSHIPS

Antisthenes had a complex network of personal relationships that influenced his life and work. His students and followers were a significant part of his life. They looked up to him not just as a teacher but as a mentor and guide. He formed close bonds with many of them, offering advice and support as they navigated their own philosophical journeys.

One of his closest relationships was with Diogenes of Sinope. Diogenes admired Antisthenes' commitment to Cynic principles and adopted a similar lifestyle. Their relationship was one of mutual respect and shared values. Diogenes often credited Antisthenes with shaping his views and inspiring his radical approach to Cynicism. This bond between teacher and student was a cornerstone of Antisthenes' personal life.

Antisthenes also had important connections with other philosophers, such as Socrates and Plato. His relationship with Socrates was foundational, as Socrates' methods and ideas profoundly influenced Antisthenes. The two shared many discussions and debates, deepening Antisthenes' understanding of virtue and ethics. With Plato, the relationship was more contentious, reflecting their different philosophical paths, but it was still marked by mutual recognition of each other's intellectual contributions.

Despite his strong philosophical convictions, Antisthenes' personal relationships were not without challenges. His blunt and direct manner could sometimes strain friendships and create conflicts. He was not one to compromise on his principles, which could make him seem rigid or unyielding. These traits sometimes made it difficult for him to maintain close personal connections outside his immediate circle of followers.

Family was another aspect of Antisthenes' personal life, though it is less documented. It is believed that his background was modest, which influenced his views on wealth and materialism. His family relationships likely shaped his early life and philosophical development, reinforcing his beliefs about the importance of virtue over material success.

ANECDOTES AND STORIES

Many anecdotes and stories about Antisthenes highlight his character and the way he lived his philosophy. One well-known story involves his reaction to a lavish banquet. When invited to a rich man's feast, Antisthenes reportedly threw away the rich food, declaring that it was more important to be free from such indulgences. This act symbolized his commitment to simplicity and self-discipline.

Another story tells of how Antisthenes dealt with a young man who wanted to study with him. Instead of welcoming the student immediately, Antisthenes made him wait and prove his dedication. The young man had to demonstrate his commitment by enduring hardships, showing that he was serious about learning. This story illustrates Antisthenes' belief in the importance of perseverance and the challenges of pursuing a virtuous life.

A famous anecdote involving Diogenes of Sinope shows the depth of Antisthenes' influence. When Diogenes approached Antisthenes to become his student, Antisthenes initially resisted. Diogenes persisted, even sitting outside Antisthenes' home and enduring insults and rejections. Eventually, Antisthenes accepted him, impressed by his determination. This story highlights the rigorous demands Antisthenes placed on those who wished to learn from him.

Antisthenes was also known for his sharp wit. In one instance, he was asked what benefit he had gained from philosophy. He replied that he had learned to live without the need for anything. This response encapsulates his belief in self-sufficiency and the idea that true happiness comes from within, not from external possessions or status.

These anecdotes and stories paint a vivid picture of Antisthenes as a person who lived his philosophy with unwavering commitment. They reveal a man who was not afraid to challenge societal norms, who demanded the highest standards from himself and his students, and who valued simplicity and virtue above all else. These stories continue to inspire and illustrate the practical application of Cynic principles.

ANTISTHENES AS A PUBLIC FIGURE

As a public figure, Antisthenes was both respected and controversial. He was a familiar sight in the Agora, Athens' bustling marketplace, where he would engage in public discussions and debates. His presence there was a testament to his belief that philosophy should be practiced openly and accessible to everyone. He saw the Agora as the perfect place to challenge people's thinking and encourage them to live more virtuous lives.

Antisthenes' public speeches were direct and often provocative. He did not shy away from criticizing those he saw as hypocritical or morally corrupt. This bluntness earned him both admiration and scorn. Some people appreciated his honesty and willingness to speak truth to power, while others saw him as rude and disrespectful. Despite the mixed reactions, Antisthenes remained steadfast in his commitment to his principles.

His role as a public figure also meant that Antisthenes was often involved in debates with other philosophers. These public debates were a way for him to test his ideas and challenge others. He enjoyed the intellectual sparring and saw it as a way to refine his own thinking. These debates were not just academic exercises but were meant to provoke thought and encourage people to examine their own lives and values.

Antisthenes' visibility in public life also made him a target for criticism. Some people accused him of being overly harsh and uncompromising. They argued that his rejection of societal norms was impractical and extreme. Antisthenes responded to these criticisms by doubling down on his beliefs, arguing that true virtue required rejecting the superficial values of society. His public stance made him a polarizing figure, but it also solidified his reputation as a dedicated philosopher.

Through his public life, Antisthenes demonstrated the practical application of Cynic principles. He showed that philosophy was not just about abstract ideas but about how one lived their life. His public presence was a constant reminder of his commitment to simplicity, virtue, and self-sufficiency. Even though his methods were sometimes controversial, they were effective in promoting his ideas and challenging others to think more deeply about their own lives.

CHALLENGES AND CONTROVERSIES

Antisthenes faced many challenges and controversies throughout his life. His radical ideas and lifestyle often put him at odds with the mainstream values of Athenian society. People who were deeply attached to wealth, status, and luxury found his rejection of these things baffling and even threatening. His philosophy challenged the foundations of their way of life, leading to friction and conflict.

One of the significant challenges Antisthenes faced was the public's misunderstanding of his intentions. Many people saw his lifestyle as unnecessarily harsh or even hypocritical. They questioned why someone would choose to live in poverty and discomfort when they didn't have to. Antisthenes had to constantly explain and defend his beliefs, emphasizing that his choices were about living a virtuous life, not about seeking approval or admiration.

Antisthenes also faced opposition from other philosophers. His blunt criticism of the Sophists, who were known for their rhetorical skills and relativistic approach to truth, earned him many enemies. He accused them of valuing style over substance and of being more interested in winning arguments than in seeking genuine knowledge. These criticisms led to heated debates and sometimes strained relationships with other thinkers.

Another controversy involved Antisthenes' views on traditional religious practices. He believed that true piety was about living a virtuous life, not about performing rituals or making sacrifices. This view was controversial because it challenged the established religious customs of the time. Antisthenes argued that many religious practices were superficial and did not contribute to a person's moral development.

Despite these challenges, Antisthenes remained unwavering in his commitment to his principles. He saw the controversies and criticisms as opportunities to clarify and strengthen his ideas. Instead of backing down, he used these challenges to further articulate his vision of a life of virtue and simplicity. His resilience in the face of opposition demonstrated his dedication to living according to his beliefs, no matter the cost.

DEATH AND LEGACY

Antisthenes' death marked the end of an era, but his legacy continued to influence generations of philosophers and thinkers. He passed away after a long life dedicated to the pursuit of virtue and the rejection of materialism. His teachings had already made a significant impact on his students and followers, ensuring that his ideas would live on.

The legacy of Antisthenes is most evident in the Cynic school of philosophy, which he founded. His principles of simplicity, self-sufficiency, and virtue became the core of Cynic thought. Figures like Diogenes and Crates carried forward his teachings, each adding their interpretations and practices. The Cynic tradition continued to challenge societal norms and inspire individuals to live more authentically.

Antisthenes' influence extended beyond the Cynic school. His ideas about virtue and self-discipline resonated with Stoic philosophers like Zeno of Citium, who incorporated Cynic principles into their own teachings. The Stoic emphasis on living in accordance with nature and focusing on inner virtues can be traced back to Antisthenes' foundational ideas.

In addition to his impact on philosophy, Antisthenes' legacy can be seen in his approach to teaching and living philosophy. He demonstrated that philosophy was not just an intellectual exercise but a way of life. His commitment to living according to his principles inspired others to do the same.

This practical approach to philosophy influenced many who came after him, including early Christian thinkers and modern advocates of simple living.

Today, Antisthenes is remembered as a pioneering figure in Western philosophy. His teachings continue to inspire those who seek to live a life of integrity and simplicity. His emphasis on virtue and self-sufficiency remains relevant in contemporary discussions about ethics and the good life. The legacy of Antisthenes is a testament to the enduring power of his ideas and the impact of a life lived in accordance with one's principles.

ANTISTHENES' LEGACY

IMMEDIATE IMPACT ON ANCIENT PHILOSOPHY

Antisthenes' ideas made waves in ancient philosophy right away. His focus on living a simple, virtuous life was a direct challenge to the more materialistic and pleasure-seeking attitudes of the time. Many people found his teachings refreshing and inspiring, and he quickly gathered a group of dedicated followers.

These followers, inspired by his teachings, began to spread his ideas throughout Athens and beyond. They practiced his principles of self-sufficiency and virtue, living in ways that set them apart from the rest of society. This new approach to philosophy caught the attention of other thinkers and sparked a lot of discussions about what it meant to live a good life.

Antisthenes' impact was also felt in the way he engaged with other philosophers. He wasn't afraid to challenge the

Sophists, who were known for their rhetorical skills and often relativistic views on truth. His debates with them were fierce and brought a lot of attention to his ideas. These public debates helped establish his reputation as a serious and influential philosopher.

Another immediate impact of Antisthenes' work was on the development of Cynicism. His principles laid the groundwork for this new school of thought, which would become known for its emphasis on living in accordance with nature and rejecting societal norms. His most famous student, Diogenes, took these ideas to new extremes, further spreading the influence of Antisthenes.

The immediate impact of Antisthenes on ancient philosophy was significant. He introduced new ideas about virtue and simplicity that challenged the status quo. His teachings inspired a new generation of philosophers who continued to develop and spread his ideas. This immediate influence set the stage for the lasting legacy that Antisthenes would leave on the world of philosophy.

INFLUENCE ON HELLENISTIC SCHOOLS

Antisthenes' teachings continued to influence philosophy long after his death, particularly during the Hellenistic period. His emphasis on virtue and self-discipline resonated with many thinkers, especially those involved in the development of Stoicism. Zeno of Citium, the founder of Stoicism, was deeply influenced by the principles of Cynicism that Antisthenes had established.

Zeno studied under Crates of Thebes, who was a direct student of Antisthenes. This connection ensured that the core ideas of Cynicism, such as living according to nature and practicing self-control, were incorporated into Stoic philosophy. The Stoics expanded on these ideas, creating a more structured system of thought, but the influence of Antisthenes was always present.

Epicureanism, another Hellenistic school, also felt the impact of Antisthenes' ideas. Although the Epicureans had a different approach to happiness, focusing on the pursuit of pleasure and the avoidance of pain, they respected the Cynic emphasis on simple living. The dialogue between these schools helped to enrich philosophical discussions during this period.

Antisthenes' influence extended to the ethical teachings of the Hellenistic schools. His focus on virtue as the highest good became a central theme in many philosophical discussions. The emphasis on ethical living and personal integrity that he promoted was adopted and adapted by various thinkers, contributing to the broader discourse on ethics in the ancient world.

The Hellenistic period was marked by a rich exchange of ideas, and Antisthenes' contributions played a significant role in shaping this intellectual landscape. His teachings on virtue, simplicity, and self-sufficiency provided a foundation for further philosophical exploration and debate, influencing a wide range of schools and thinkers.

REFERENCES IN LATER PHILOSOPHICAL WORKS

Antisthenes' impact on philosophy can be seen in the way later philosophers referenced his work. His ideas were cited and discussed by many thinkers, showing the lasting relevance of his teachings. These references highlight how his contributions continued to shape philosophical thought long after his death.

Plato and Aristotle, two of the most prominent philosophers of ancient Greece, both engaged with Antisthenes' ideas. While they had their own distinct philosophical systems, they acknowledged the importance of his emphasis on virtue and ethical living. Their discussions of ethics often included critiques and expansions of Antisthenes' views, demonstrating his influence on their work.

The Roman Stoics, such as Seneca, Epictetus, and Marcus Aurelius, also drew on Antisthenes' ideas. They admired his commitment to virtue and his rejection of materialism. Epictetus, in particular, often referred to Cynic principles in his teachings, showing how Antisthenes' ideas were integrated into Stoic thought. These references helped to keep Antisthenes' legacy alive and relevant.

During the Renaissance, when classical texts were rediscovered and studied anew, Antisthenes' ideas once again gained prominence. Humanist scholars explored his teachings on virtue and simplicity, finding inspiration in his commitment to living a principled life. These Renaissance thinkers saw Antisthenes as a model of philosophical integrity, and his ideas influenced the ethical debates of the time.

In modern times, philosophers continue to reference Antisthenes when discussing the history of ethics and the development of Cynicism. His teachings are seen as foundational for understanding the evolution of philosophical thought on virtue and the good life. By tracing the references to Antisthenes in later works, we can see how his ideas have endured and continued to inspire new generations of thinkers.

CONTRIBUTION TO ETHICAL THOUGHT

Antisthenes made significant contributions to ethical thought, particularly through his emphasis on virtue as the highest good. He believed that living a virtuous life was the key to happiness and that external factors like wealth or fame were irrelevant. This focus on inner goodness over external success was a radical departure from the more materialistic views of his time.

One of Antisthenes' key contributions was his idea that virtue could be taught and learned. He argued that anyone could achieve virtue through education and self-discipline. This democratization of virtue challenged the notion that only certain people, such as the wealthy or noble-born, could live good lives. Antisthenes believed that virtue was accessible to all, regardless of their social status.

Antisthenes introduced the idea that living in harmony with nature was crucial for a virtuous life. He believed that societal norms and conventions often diverted people from their true nature, leading to lives of excess and vice. By rejecting these artificial constructs and embracing a more natural way of living, individuals could achieve true happiness and fulfillment.

His emphasis on self-sufficiency and simplicity as key components of a virtuous life was another important contribution. Antisthenes taught that by minimizing one's desires and focusing on what was truly necessary, individuals could achieve greater freedom and contentment. This idea was influential in the development of Cynicism and later Stoicism, both of which emphasized the importance of self-control and living simply.

Antisthenes' contributions to ethical thought have had a lasting impact. His teachings on virtue, simplicity, and living according to nature continue to resonate with people today. By challenging the conventional values of his time and promoting a more principled way of living, Antisthenes helped to shape the ethical discourse of the ancient world and beyond.

ROLE IN THE HISTORY OF PHILOSOPHY

Antisthenes holds a significant place in the history of philosophy. As a student of Socrates and a contemporary of Plato, he was part of a transformative period in Greek thought. His contributions helped to shape the development of Western philosophy, particularly through his influence on the Cynic and Stoic schools.

One of Antisthenes' key roles was as a bridge between Socratic and Cynic philosophy. He took the teachings of Socrates and applied them in a way that emphasized practical ethics and the rejection of societal norms. This approach laid the groundwork for Cynicism, which would become a major philosophical movement in its own right.

Antisthenes' focus on virtue and ethical living also influenced other philosophical traditions. His ideas about self-sufficiency and living in accordance with nature were foundational for Stoicism, one of the most enduring schools of ancient philosophy. The Stoics took Antisthenes' principles and developed them into a comprehensive system of thought that has continued to be influential for centuries.

In addition to his influence on specific schools of philosophy, Antisthenes' emphasis on practical ethics has had a broader impact. His teachings challenged the idea that philosophy was purely theoretical and demonstrated that it could be a guide for everyday living. This practical approach to philosophy has been adopted by many thinkers throughout history, from the early Christians to modern philosophers.

Antisthenes' role in the history of philosophy is also evident in the way his ideas have been referenced and discussed by later thinkers. His contributions to discussions on virtue, simplicity, and ethical living have been acknowledged and built upon by philosophers across different eras. This ongoing engagement with his ideas highlights the enduring relevance of his work.

Overall, Antisthenes played a crucial role in the development of Western philosophy. His teachings helped to shape key philosophical movements and influenced the way people think about ethics and the good life. His legacy continues to be felt in the ongoing discourse on how to live a virtuous and meaningful life.

REVIVAL IN MODERN TIMES

Antisthenes' ideas have seen a revival in modern times, particularly as people seek alternatives to materialism and consumerism. His emphasis on simplicity, virtue, and self-sufficiency resonates with contemporary movements that advocate for minimalism and sustainable living. These modern interpretations show how his ancient teachings remain relevant today.

The minimalist movement, which promotes living with fewer possessions and focusing on what truly matters, echoes Antisthenes' principles. Modern minimalists advocate for reducing material excess and finding happiness in simplicity, much like Antisthenes did. His ideas about self-sufficiency and rejecting societal norms align closely with the values of this movement.

Environmentalism is another area where Antisthenes' teachings have found new expression. The emphasis on living according to nature and minimizing harm to the environment is a core tenet of many environmental movements. Antisthenes' belief in simplicity and rejecting unnecessary luxuries fits well with the push for sustainable living and reducing one's ecological footprint.

In psychology, the focus on authenticity and self-awareness in Antisthenes' philosophy parallels modern therapeutic practices. Approaches such as mindfulness and existential therapy encourage individuals to live true to their values and reject societal pressures, reflecting the Cynic emphasis on inner virtue and self-discipline. These practices help people achieve greater well-being by aligning their lives with their core beliefs.

Modern social critics also draw on Antisthenes' ideas to challenge consumerism and the superficial values of contemporary society. By questioning the importance of wealth, status, and material possessions, these critics promote a more meaningful and ethical way of living. Antisthenes' legacy is evident in their calls for a return to simpler, more virtuous lives.

The revival of Antisthenes' ideas in modern times demonstrates their enduring relevance. His teachings offer valuable insights for addressing contemporary challenges and provide a framework for living a more authentic and ethical life. By looking to the past, modern thinkers can find inspiration in Antisthenes' philosophy and apply its principles to today's world.

ANTISTHENES IN POPULAR CULTURE

Antisthenes' influence extends beyond philosophy and into popular culture. His ideas about virtue, simplicity, and living according to nature have inspired various forms of artistic and literary expression. These cultural representations help to keep his legacy alive and introduce his teachings to new audiences.

Antisthenes' principles have been explored in both fiction and non-fiction literature. Authors who write about minimalism and simple living often reference his ideas. His emphasis on self-sufficiency and rejecting societal norms provides a rich source of inspiration for stories about characters who choose to live differently from the mainstream. These narratives help to illustrate the practical applications of his philosophy.

Film and television have also portrayed characters and themes influenced by Antisthenes' teachings. Movies that focus on individuals who reject materialism and seek a more meaningful life often echo Cynic principles. These portrayals resonate with audiences who are looking for alternatives to the consumerist culture and inspire them to consider different ways of living.

Art, too, has been influenced by Antisthenes' ideas. Visual artists who explore themes of simplicity, nature, and ethical living draw on the principles he espoused. Their works challenge viewers to reflect on their own values and consider the importance of virtue over material success. This artistic engagement with Cynic philosophy helps to bring its ideas into contemporary cultural conversations.

Antisthenes' legacy is also evident in the growing interest in mindfulness and wellness practices. These movements often emphasize living in the present moment, reducing stress, and focusing on what truly matters—ideas that align closely with Cynic philosophy. By promoting a more intentional and thoughtful way of living, these practices help to spread Antisthenes' teachings in a modern context.

Through its presence in popular culture, Antisthenes' philosophy continues to reach and influence new generations. His ideas about virtue, simplicity, and living according to nature remain relevant and inspiring. By engaging with these cultural representations, people can discover the timeless wisdom of Antisthenes and apply it to their own lives.

MODERN INTERPRETATIONS AND RELEVANCE

CONTEMPORARY PHILOSOPHICAL VIEWS

Antisthenes' philosophy continues to hold significance in contemporary philosophical discussions. Modern philosophers often revisit his ideas about virtue and self-sufficiency. These principles remain relevant as they address timeless questions about what it means to live a good life. Antisthenes' focus on living in accordance with nature and rejecting societal norms resonates with those seeking authenticity in a rapidly changing world.

Philosophers today also examine Antisthenes' contributions to ethical thought. His belief that virtue is the only true good challenges modern materialistic values. By emphasizing inner goodness over external success, Antisthenes provides a counter-narrative to the pursuit of wealth and status. This perspective invites a reevaluation of what constitutes a meaningful life in contemporary society.

Another aspect of Antisthenes' philosophy that attracts modern attention is his critique of conventional wisdom. He encouraged questioning established norms and beliefs, a practice that remains crucial in philosophical inquiry. This critical approach helps individuals and societies to think more deeply about their values and practices, promoting intellectual and moral growth.

The practical nature of Antisthenes' teachings also appeals to contemporary thinkers. His ideas are not just abstract theories but actionable guidelines for living. This practical application makes his philosophy accessible and relevant to people seeking concrete ways to improve their lives. Modern philosophers appreciate this aspect of his work as it bridges the gap between theory and practice.

In contemporary philosophical discussions, Antisthenes is often seen as a precursor to later movements like Stoicism and existentialism. His emphasis on living authentically and according to one's principles is echoed in these traditions. By studying Antisthenes, modern philosophers gain insight into the roots of these ideas and their ongoing relevance.

ANTISTHENES IN MODERN ETHICAL DEBATES

Antisthenes' ideas play a significant role in modern ethical debates. His focus on virtue as the highest good challenges contemporary views on success and happiness. In a world often driven by materialism and consumerism, Antisthenes' teachings offer a refreshing perspective that prioritizes ethical living over wealth and status.

One area where Antisthenes' influence is evident is in discussions about ethical consumerism. His emphasis on simplicity and self-sufficiency aligns with movements that promote mindful consumption and sustainability. By advocating for a lifestyle that minimizes harm and excess, Antisthenes' philosophy supports ethical choices that benefit both individuals and society.

Antisthenes' critique of societal norms also resonates in debates about social justice. His rejection of superficial values and his call for living according to nature challenge systems of inequality and oppression. Modern activists and thinkers draw on his ideas to advocate for a more just and equitable society, one that values individuals for their character rather than their social status or material possessions.

In the realm of personal ethics, Antisthenes' teachings encourage self-examination and integrity. His belief that true happiness comes from within rather than from external sources invites individuals to reflect on their values and actions. This introspective approach is vital in developing a coherent and meaningful ethical framework in today's complex world.

Antisthenes' ideas also contribute to the discourse on mental health and well-being. His emphasis on self-discipline and living in harmony with one's values can help individuals find balance and fulfillment. By focusing on inner virtue and rejecting external pressures, people can achieve greater peace and contentment, which are essential components of mental health.

INFLUENCE ON MODERN MINIMALISM

Antisthenes' philosophy has had a significant impact on the modern minimalist movement. His teachings on simplicity and self-sufficiency align closely with the principles of minimalism, which advocates for living with less to focus on what truly matters. Modern minimalists find inspiration in Antisthenes' rejection of material excess and his emphasis on inner virtue.

Minimalism, as a lifestyle, promotes the idea of reducing possessions and distractions to create space for more meaningful activities and relationships. This approach mirrors Antisthenes' belief that true happiness comes from living a simple life. By eliminating unnecessary belongings and focusing on essentials, minimalists strive to achieve a sense of peace and contentment, similar to what Antisthenes advocated.

Antisthenes' teachings also influence minimalism's ethical dimension. Modern minimalists often emphasize sustainability and ethical consumption, principles that resonate with Antisthenes' focus on living in accordance with nature. By choosing to live simply, minimalists aim to reduce their environmental impact and promote a more sustainable way of life, reflecting Antisthenes' values.

The minimalist movement also embraces the idea of self-sufficiency, a core principle of Antisthenes' philosophy. Minimalists seek to reduce their dependence on material goods and external validation, fostering a sense of independence and self-reliance. This approach encourages individuals to find fulfillment within themselves, aligning with Antisthenes' belief in the importance of inner virtue.

Antisthenes' influence on modern minimalism highlights the enduring relevance of his ideas. By promoting simplicity, ethical living, and self-sufficiency, minimalism continues the legacy of Antisthenes in a contemporary context. His teachings provide a timeless framework for living a meaningful and fulfilling life, free from the distractions of material excess.

RELEVANCE TO MODERN SOCIAL CRITIQUE

Antisthenes' philosophy is highly relevant to modern social critique. His rejection of societal norms and materialism offers a powerful framework for challenging contemporary social structures and values. By questioning the status quo, Antisthenes' ideas encourage critical thinking and inspire movements for social change.

One area where Antisthenes' influence is evident is in the critique of consumer culture. Modern social critics draw on his rejection of material wealth to challenge the pervasive consumerism that dominates society. They argue that the relentless pursuit of material goods leads to environmental degradation and social inequality, echoing Antisthenes' concerns about the corrupting influence of wealth.

Antisthenes' emphasis on living according to nature also resonates with critiques of modern industrial society. Environmental activists use his ideas to advocate for more sustainable and ecologically harmonious ways of living. By promoting simplicity and self-sufficiency, Antisthenes' philosophy supports efforts to reduce human impact on the environment and create a more sustainable future.

In the realm of social justice, Antisthenes' teachings challenge systems of power and privilege. His belief in the inherent worth of individuals, regardless of their social status, aligns with modern movements that fight against discrimination and inequality. Activists draw on his ideas to advocate for a society that values people for their character and actions rather than their wealth or background.

Antisthenes' critique of conventional wisdom also supports efforts to promote independent thinking and resist conformity. His emphasis on questioning established norms encourages individuals to think critically about the world around them and to seek their own path. This approach is particularly relevant in an age of mass media and social pressure, where independent thought is often stifled.

The relevance of Antisthenes' philosophy to modern social critique underscores its enduring power. His ideas provide a foundation for challenging societal norms and advocating for a more just and sustainable world. By drawing on his teachings, modern critics can find inspiration and guidance in their efforts to create positive social change.

ANTISTHENES AND MODERN EDUCATION

Antisthenes' ideas have significant implications for modern education. His emphasis on virtue and practical ethics suggests a model of education that goes beyond academic knowledge to include character development and moral integrity. This holistic approach to education is increasingly relevant in today's complex and interconnected world.

One aspect of Antisthenes' influence on education is the focus on critical thinking and questioning. He believed that true knowledge came from challenging assumptions and seeking deeper understanding. Modern educators can draw on this principle to encourage students to think critically and question the information they receive, fostering a more inquisitive and independent mindset.

Antisthenes also emphasized the importance of living according to one's values, an idea that can be integrated into character education programs. By teaching students about virtue and ethical living, educators can help them develop a strong moral compass. This approach prepares students to navigate ethical dilemmas and make principled decisions in their personal and professional lives.

The practical nature of Antisthenes' philosophy also supports experiential learning. He believed that philosophy should be practiced, not just studied. Modern educational approaches that emphasize hands-on learning and real-world applications can benefit from this perspective. By engaging students in activities that require them to apply their knowledge and skills, educators can make learning more relevant and impactful.

Antisthenes' commitment to simplicity and self-sufficiency can also inform educational practices. Teaching students about sustainable living and the value of minimalism can help them develop a more balanced and mindful approach to life. This perspective encourages students to prioritize well-being and ethical living over material success, aligning with the principles of Antisthenes' philosophy.

By incorporating Antisthenes' ideas into modern education, educators can create a more holistic and values-driven approach to learning. His emphasis on virtue, critical thinking, and practical ethics provides a timeless framework for preparing students to lead meaningful and principled lives.

LEGACY IN CONTEMPORARY PHILOSOPHY

Antisthenes' legacy continues to shape contemporary philosophy. His ideas about virtue, simplicity, and self-sufficiency remain influential in ongoing philosophical discussions. Modern philosophers often revisit his teachings to explore their relevance to current ethical and existential questions.

One area where Antisthenes' legacy is particularly strong is in the field of virtue ethics. His belief that virtue is the highest good has inspired many contemporary ethicists who emphasize the importance of character and moral integrity. This focus on virtue provides a counterpoint to more rule-based or consequentialist approaches to ethics, offering a holistic view of moral development.

Antisthenes' critique of materialism also resonates with contemporary philosophical debates about the nature of happiness and well-being. His emphasis on inner goodness and the rejection of external wealth challenges the dominant narratives of consumer culture. Philosophers today explore these ideas to argue for more sustainable and fulfilling ways of living.

The practical nature of Antisthenes' philosophy has also influenced existentialist thought. His focus on living authentically and according to one's principles aligns with existentialist themes of individual freedom and responsibility. By examining Antisthenes' teachings, contemporary philosophers gain insights into the roots of existentialist ideas and their application to modern life.

Antisthenes' legacy is also evident in the continued relevance of Cynicism. Modern interpretations of Cynic philosophy draw on his teachings to address contemporary social and ethical issues. The emphasis on questioning societal norms and living a simple, virtuous life provides a framework for critiquing modern values and promoting ethical living.

The enduring influence of Antisthenes in contemporary philosophy highlights the timeless nature of his ideas. His teachings continue to inspire and challenge philosophers, offering valuable insights into the pursuit of a meaningful and ethical life. By engaging with his legacy, modern thinkers can find guidance and inspiration in their philosophical explorations.

FUTURE DIRECTIONS OF ANTISTHENES' THOUGHT

The future of Antisthenes' thought looks promising as his ideas continue to find new relevance in a rapidly changing world. Scholars and thinkers are likely to keep exploring his philosophy to address emerging ethical, social, and environmental challenges. The timeless principles of virtue, simplicity, and self-sufficiency that he championed offer a rich source of inspiration for future generations.

One potential direction for the continued exploration of Antisthenes' thought is in the field of environmental ethics. As concerns about climate change and sustainability grow, his emphasis on living in harmony with nature becomes increasingly relevant. Future philosophers and activists may draw on his teachings to develop more sustainable practices and promote a deeper respect for the natural world.

Antisthenes' ideas have the potential to influence future educational reforms. As the demand for holistic and values-based education grows, his emphasis on virtue and practical ethics could shape new teaching and learning approaches. By incorporating his principles into educational curricula, future educators can help students develop the character and skills needed to navigate a complex world.

In the realm of technology and digital culture, Antisthenes' critique of materialism and focus on self-sufficiency offer valuable insights. As society becomes increasingly dependent on technology and digital media, his teachings can provide a counterbalance that encourages mindful consumption and ethical use of technology. Future thinkers might explore how his ideas can foster a more balanced and intentional digital life.

Social and political philosophy could also benefit from renewed attention to Antisthenes' ideas. His critique of societal norms and advocacy for ethical living provide a framework for addressing issues of inequality, justice, and community. Future philosophers and activists may draw on his teachings to develop new approaches for creating more just and equitable societies.

The future of Antisthenes' thought is bright, with many potential avenues for exploration and application. His timeless principles offer valuable guidance for addressing contemporary challenges and promoting a more ethical and fulfilling way of life. As future generations continue to engage with his ideas, Antisthenes' legacy will undoubtedly endure and evolve.

CONCLUSION

SUMMARY OF ANTISTHENES' LIFE

Antisthenes was born in Athens and became one of the most influential philosophers of his time. He was a student of Socrates, and his teachings were deeply shaped by his mentor's ideas. Antisthenes believed in living a life of virtue and simplicity, rejecting material wealth and societal norms. He was known for his blunt and direct manner, often challenging others to rethink their values and beliefs.

Throughout his life, Antisthenes practiced what he preached. He lived modestly, focusing on self-discipline and inner goodness. His public discussions in places like the Agora made him a well-known figure in Athens. He gathered a group of dedicated followers who were inspired by his commitment to virtue and his practical approach to philosophy.

Antisthenes' influence extended beyond his immediate circle of students. His ideas laid the groundwork for the Cynic school of

CONCLUSION

philosophy, which emphasized living in accordance with nature and rejecting superficial values. His teachings also influenced other philosophical traditions, including Stoicism, which further developed his ideas about virtue and self-sufficiency.

Despite facing criticism and opposition, Antisthenes remained steadfast in his beliefs. His determination to live according to his principles made him a respected and sometimes controversial figure. His life was a testament to the power of living authentically and ethically, regardless of societal pressures.

Antisthenes' legacy continues to be felt today. His ideas about virtue, simplicity, and self-sufficiency have inspired countless thinkers and movements. His life serves as an example of how philosophy can be a practical guide for living a meaningful and principled life.

KEY PHILOSOPHICAL CONTRIBUTIONS

Antisthenes made several key contributions to philosophy that continue to resonate today. One of his most important ideas was that virtue is the only true good. He believed that living a virtuous life was the most important goal one could achieve. This emphasis on inner goodness over external success was revolutionary and challenged the materialistic values of his time.

Another significant contribution was his idea of self-sufficiency. Antisthenes taught that true happiness comes from being independent and not relying on external things. He believed that by minimizing desires and focusing on what is truly necessary, people could achieve greater freedom and contentment. This idea influenced the development of Cynicism and Stoicism, both of which emphasize self-control and living simply.

Antisthenes also introduced the concept of living according to nature. He argued that societal norms and conventions often led people away from their true nature and into lives of excess and vice. By rejecting these artificial constructs and returning to a more natural way of living, people could find true happiness and fulfillment. This principle became a cornerstone of Cynic philosophy.

His practical approach to philosophy was another key contribution. Antisthenes believed that philosophy should be a guide for everyday living, not just an intellectual exercise. He emphasized the importance of applying philosophical principles in daily life, demonstrating that philosophy could be both practical and transformative.

Antisthenes' teachings also included a strong critique of conventional wisdom and societal values. He encouraged questioning established norms and beliefs, promoting critical thinking and intellectual independence. This critical approach remains an essential aspect of philosophical inquiry and has influenced many thinkers throughout history.

LASTING IMPACT ON PHILOSOPHY

The lasting impact of Antisthenes on philosophy is significant. His ideas about virtue, simplicity, and self-sufficiency have continued to influence philosophical thought for centuries. His emphasis on practical ethics and living

CONCLUSION

according to nature laid the groundwork for the development of several major philosophical traditions.

One of the most notable impacts of Antisthenes' philosophy is its influence on Cynicism. As the founder of the Cynic school, his teachings shaped the movement's core principles. Cynicism's focus on living a simple, virtuous life in accordance with nature can be directly traced back to Antisthenes' ideas. His influence ensured that Cynicism remained a significant philosophical tradition in the ancient world.

Antisthenes' ideas also had a profound impact on Stoicism. Zeno of Citium, the founder of Stoicism, was heavily influenced by Cynic principles. The Stoic emphasis on virtue, self-discipline, and living in harmony with nature reflects Antisthenes' teachings. By integrating these ideas into a comprehensive philosophical system, Stoicism became one of the most enduring schools of ancient philosophy.

His critique of societal norms and focus on inner goodness also influenced early Christian thought. Many early Christian thinkers adopted Cynic practices of simplicity and asceticism, seeing them as a path to spiritual purity. Antisthenes' emphasis on virtue over material wealth resonated with Christian teachings about humility and self-denial.

In modern times, Antisthenes' philosophy continues to be relevant. His ideas about living a virtuous life, questioning societal norms, and finding happiness in simplicity resonate with contemporary movements that challenge consumerism and advocate for ethical living. His teachings provide a timeless framework for addressing the ethical and existential challenges of the modern world.

CONCLUSION

Antisthenes' lasting impact on philosophy is a testament to the enduring power of his ideas. His contributions have shaped the development of ethical thought and continue to inspire philosophers and thinkers across different eras and cultures.

RELEVANCE TO MODERN TIMES

Antisthenes' philosophy remains highly relevant in modern times, offering valuable insights for addressing contemporary challenges. His emphasis on virtue, simplicity, and self-sufficiency provides a powerful counter-narrative to the materialism and consumerism that dominate modern society.

One way Antisthenes' ideas are relevant today is through the minimalist movement. Modern minimalists advocate for living with fewer possessions and focusing on what truly matters, echoing Antisthenes' teachings on simplicity and self-sufficiency. By rejecting material excess and prioritizing well-being, minimalists strive to create more meaningful and fulfilling lives.

Antisthenes' philosophy also resonates with environmentalism. His emphasis on living according to nature and rejecting unnecessary luxuries aligns with contemporary efforts to promote sustainable living. Environmental activists draw on his principles to advocate for lifestyles that minimize harm to the planet and foster a deeper connection with the natural world.

In the realm of mental health and well-being, Antisthenes' teachings offer valuable guidance. His focus on self-discipline and inner virtue encourages individuals to find happiness within themselves rather than seeking it through external sources. This introspective approach is essential for developing resilience and achieving a balanced, contented life.

Antisthenes' critique of societal norms and emphasis on questioning established beliefs are also relevant to modern social critique. His philosophy encourages critical thinking and intellectual independence, empowering individuals to challenge the status quo and advocate for positive change. This critical approach is vital in addressing issues of inequality, injustice, and environmental degradation.

The relevance of Antisthenes' philosophy to modern times highlights its enduring power. His teachings provide a timeless framework for living a virtuous, meaningful life and offer valuable insights for addressing the ethical and existential challenges of today's world.

REFLECTIONS ON ANTISTHENES' TEACHINGS

Reflecting on Antisthenes' teachings reveals their profound wisdom and enduring relevance. His emphasis on virtue as the highest good challenges us to reconsider our values and priorities. In a world often driven by materialism and external success, Antisthenes reminds us that true happiness comes from within and is rooted in living a principled life.

His teachings on simplicity and self-sufficiency encourage us to adopt more mindful and intentional lifestyles. By focusing on what is truly necessary and minimizing our desires, we can achieve greater freedom and contentment. This approach not only benefits our well-being but also promotes sustainability and ethical living.

CONCLUSION

Antisthenes' critique of societal norms invites us to question the conventions and expectations that shape our lives. By challenging established beliefs and practices, we can develop a deeper understanding of ourselves and the world around us. This critical approach fosters intellectual independence and encourages us to think more deeply about our values and actions.

His practical approach to philosophy demonstrates that ethical living is not just an abstract concept but a way of life. Antisthenes' teachings provide actionable guidelines for navigating the complexities of modern life. By applying his principles in our daily lives, we can cultivate virtue, self-discipline, and inner peace.

Reflecting on Antisthenes' teachings also highlights the importance of living authentically. His commitment to living according to his principles, despite societal pressures, inspires us to be true to ourselves and our values. This authenticity is essential for achieving a meaningful and fulfilling life.

Antisthenes' teachings offer valuable insights for living a virtuous, meaningful life. His emphasis on virtue, simplicity, and critical thinking provides a timeless framework for addressing contemporary challenges and achieving inner peace and fulfillment.

IMPORTANCE OF CYNICISM TODAY

Cynicism, as founded by Antisthenes, remains important in today's world. Its emphasis on living in accordance with nature, rejecting material excess, and focusing on inner

CONCLUSION

virtue offers a powerful alternative to the dominant values of consumerism and superficial success.

In a world where material wealth and status are often seen as the ultimate goals, Cynicism challenges us to reconsider what truly matters. By rejecting societal norms that prioritize external success, Cynicism encourages us to focus on developing our character and living ethically. This shift in perspective can lead to greater happiness and fulfillment.

Cynicism also promotes a more sustainable way of living. Its emphasis on simplicity and self-sufficiency aligns with contemporary efforts to reduce consumption and minimize our environmental impact. By adopting Cynic principles, we can contribute to a more sustainable future and foster a deeper connection with the natural world.

The critical approach of Cynicism is particularly relevant in an age of mass media and social pressure. Cynicism encourages us to question established norms and think independently. This intellectual independence is crucial for navigating the complexities of modern life and making informed, ethical decisions.

Cynicism's focus on inner virtue and self-discipline also supports mental health and well-being. By prioritizing inner goodness over external validation, Cynicism helps us develop resilience and find contentment within ourselves. This introspective approach is essential for achieving a balanced and fulfilling life.

The importance of Cynicism today lies in its ability to challenge the dominant values of consumerism and superficial success. Its emphasis on virtue, simplicity, and critical

CONCLUSION

thinking provides a valuable framework for living a meaningful and ethical life in the modern world.

FUTURE STUDY AND EXPLORATION

The future study and exploration of Antisthenes' thought hold great promise. As contemporary challenges evolve, his teachings offer valuable insights for addressing ethical, social, and environmental issues. Scholars and thinkers will continue to explore and expand upon his ideas, ensuring their relevance for future generations.

One area of future exploration is the application of Antisthenes' principles to environmental ethics. As concerns about climate change and sustainability grow, his emphasis on living in harmony with nature becomes increasingly important. Future philosophers and activists can draw on his teachings to develop more sustainable practices and promote a deeper respect for the natural world.

Antisthenes' ideas have the potential to shape future educational reforms. As the demand for holistic and values-based education increases, his emphasis on virtue and practical ethics can inspire new teaching and learning methods. By incorporating his principles into educational curricula, future educators can help students develop the character and skills needed to navigate a complex world.

In the realm of technology and digital culture, Antisthenes' critique of materialism and focus on self-sufficiency offer valuable insights. As society becomes increasingly reliant on technology and digital media, his teachings can provide a counterbalance, encouraging mindful consumption and ethical use of technology. Future thinkers might explore how his ideas can foster a more balanced and intentional digital life.

Social and political philosophy could also benefit from renewed attention to Antisthenes' ideas. His critique of societal norms and advocacy for ethical living offer a framework for addressing issues of inequality, justice, and community. Future philosophers and activists may draw on his teachings to develop new approaches for creating more just and equitable societies.

The future study and exploration of Antisthenes' thought hold great potential for addressing contemporary challenges and promoting ethical living. His timeless principles offer valuable guidance for future generations, ensuring that his legacy will continue to inspire and inform for years to come.

GLOSSARY

Agoge - A leading or guidance.

Aidos - A sense of shame or humility.

Antisthenes - A Greek philosopher and student of Socrates who founded the Cynic school of thought.

Arete - Excellence or virtue.

Asceticism - A lifestyle characterized by abstinence from worldly pleasures.

Ataraxia - A state of serene calmness.

Autarkeia - Self-sufficiency.

Cynicism - A philosophy advocating for virtue and simplicity.

Diogenes - A prominent Cynic philosopher and follower of Antisthenes.

GLOSSARY

Dogma - A principle or set of principles laid down by an authority.

Egoism - An ethical theory that treats self-interest as the foundation of morality.

Elenchus - Socratic method of eliciting truth through questioning.

Ethics - Moral principles that govern behavior.

Eudaimonia - Human flourishing or happiness.

Eudaimonism - The ethical system that bases moral value on the likelihood of actions producing happiness.

Hellenistic - Relating to Greek history, culture, or art after Alexander the Great.

Hipparchia - A female Cynic philosopher and follower of Antisthenes.

Hybris - Excessive pride or self-confidence.

Isonomia - Equality of political rights.

Logismos - Rational calculation or reasoning.

Logos - Reason or principle.

Materialism - A tendency to consider material possessions and physical comfort as more important than spiritual values.

Megalopsychia - Greatness of soul.

Metaphysics - The branch of philosophy that deals with the first principles of things.

GLOSSARY

Minimalism - A lifestyle of simplicity and minimal material possessions.

Nomos - Law or custom.

Ontology - The branch of metaphysics dealing with the nature of being.

Parrhesia - Frankness or boldness in speech.

Pathos - Emotion or suffering.

Phronesis - Practical wisdom.

Physis - Nature.

Plato - A student of Socrates and a contemporary of Antisthenes.

Polis - A city-state in ancient Greece.

Psyche - The human soul, mind, or spirit.

Rhetoric - The art of effective or persuasive speaking or writing.

Skepticism - A skeptical attitude; doubt as to the truth of something.

Sophia - Wisdom.

Sophists - Ancient Greek teachers of philosophy, reasoning, and rhetoric.

Sophrosyne - Moderation or self-control.

Socratic Method - A form of cooperative argumentative dialogue between individuals.

Stoicism - A philosophy that teaches the development of self-control and fortitude.

GLOSSARY

Technē - Art or skill.

Telos - An ultimate object or aim.

Thebes - An ancient Greek city.

Thumos - Spirit or inner drive.

Tyche - The Greek goddess of fortune and prosperity.

Virtue - Behavior showing high moral standards.

Virtuous - Having or showing high moral standards.

Wisdom - The quality of having experience, knowledge, and good judgment.

Xenia - The ancient Greek concept of hospitality.

SUGGESTED READINGS

Beck, Martha - *Diana, Herself: An Allegory of Awakening*

Bertrand, Russell - *The History of Western Philosophy*

Epictetus - *Discourses and Selected Writings*

Hadot, Pierre - *The Inner Citadel: The Meditations of Marcus Aurelius*

Heller, Anne C. - *Ayn Rand and the World She Made*

Hesiod - *Theogony and Works and Days*

Higgins, Charlotte - *The Hemlock Cup: Socrates, Athens, and the Search for the Good Life*

Homer - *The Iliad*

Homer - *The Odyssey*

Irvine, William B. - *A Guide to the Good Life: The Ancient Art of Stoic Joy*

Johnson, Paul - *Socrates: A Man for Our Times*

SUGGESTED READINGS

Klein, Stefan - *The Science of Happiness: How Our Brains Make Us Happy - and What We Can Do to Get Happier*

Lampert, Laurence - *How Philosophy Became Socratic: A Study of Plato's Protagoras, Charmides, and Republic*

Long, A. A. - *Epictetus: A Stoic and Socratic Guide to Life*

Machiavelli, Niccolò - *The Prince*

Marcus Aurelius – *Meditations*

Plato - *The Republic*

Seneca - *Letters from a Stoic*

Xenophon – *Memorabilia*

Zweig, Stefan - *Socrates: The Philosopher*

Printed in Great Britain
by Amazon